The Presentation Book for Senior Managers

The Presentation Book for Senior Managers

An Essential Step by Step Guide to Structuring and Delivering Effective Speeches

Jay Surti

BEP BUSINESS EXPERT PRESS

The Presentation Book for Senior Managers: An Essential Step by Step Guide to Structuring and Delivering Effective Speeches

First published in 2017 by
Business Expert Press, LLC
222 East 46th Street, New York, NY 10017
www.businessexpertpress.com

ISBN-13: 978-1-63157-635-5 (paperback)
ISBN-13: 978-1-63157-636-2 (e-book)

Business Expert Corporate Communication Collection

Collection ISSN: 2156-8162 (print)
Collection ISSN: 2156-8170 (electronic)

Cover and interior design by Exeter Premedia Services Private Ltd., Chennai, India

First edition: 2017

10 9 8 7 6 5 4 3 2 1

Printed in the United States of America.

Abstract

What Is the Book About?

A comprehensive guide covering all the essential ingredients for delivering presentations that engage and persuade a professional audience. This book covers everything from planning and structuring content to delivering with confidence.

Who Is the Audience for This Book and Why Would They Buy It?

The book is for senior leaders and managers in professional organizations that need to present to a wide variety of audiences ranging from team meetings to conference speeches. The focus of the book is on engaging with the audience in a way that informs, entertains, and persuades. It is written by a former city lawyer who now helps MBA candidates master presentations—someone who understands the pitfalls of talking at audiences and providing little value.

Keywords

audience engagement, confidence, delivery, feedback, humor, mastery, storytelling, structure, stunning slides, toolkit

Contents

Introduction

This book will help you craft and deliver presentations that serve your audience, so that you stand out against mediocre presenters.

My hope is that the tools and techniques I share with you in this book will help you become more persuasive in your work and beyond, as well as inspire you to be totally comfortable being yourself when presenting. When we look at the standard of presenting that happens everyday in business, the bar is set very low, so you will easily get over that. Presenting is much more than standing up in front of a group of people and giving information. It is as much about the needs of the audience as it is about the material you share with them.

Good presenters are engaging and memorable.

What You Will Get from This Book

- Improving your communication style
- Gaining more confidence and tackling nerves
- Designing content that is memorable and relevant
- Becoming more efficient at preparing your presentations
- Creating great slides
- Discovering how to add stories to your speeches
- Being more persuasive

Whatever kind of work you do, at some point, you will have to speak in front of others. Many of you are or will be managers in your organizations—responsible for managing teams and hitting targets. Whether you see yourself as a leader or not, leadership is an important aspect of being a successful manager. You have to lead your team to meet the company's objectives. That means communicating ideas and objectives on a daily basis. As a leader, you need to engage and inspire.

It doesn't matter what you are presenting—whether it's an idea, research paper, service, or product, it all comes down to how you connect with your audience and communicate. If you have ever sat through a "death by PowerPoint" seminar or presentation or been subjected to a rambling lecture, which quite often happens when someone talks at you, then you know what a waste of time it can be. Most presenters aren't that good simply because they don't prepare well and don't practice enough. As a professional, being able to present in order to persuade and influence is a fundamental part of your job.

Giving presentations is also a good way to increase your professional profile—people associate good speaking skills with effective leaders. Great communicators command more respect and are more persuasive. You never know who may be in the room.

The basic ingredients of any presentation are:
- Content
- Structure
- Delivery

The first is the one that we find easy—*what* we want to say. This is where most average presenters focus their attention. The other two are just as important—designing the content in a way that resonates with the audience and sharing in a way that engages them. In this book, we go into a deep dive covering all three areas.

Presenters present information and appeal to reason with fact and logic. Persuaders do all of that, but also engage their audience with emotion and inspire people to act upon the knowledge shared. They make messages memorable.

My personal view is that effective presenters also need to project their authentic personality, so that people can relate to you as a person.

Preparing a presentation can be stressful for many reasons—whether that is due to pressures of time or nerves. Yet, we speak to people all day in our lives—at work and outside, so why then does panic set in when we have to factor in a live audience? Fear of speaking can be a huge hurdle to overcome. Some people will do anything to avoid it. It's an irrational fear.

It doesn't have to be like that. Speaking in front of audiences of whatever size is something that can be learned. Trust me, I can speak from experience. I had a 17-year career in law as a litigator, and yet, for much of that time, I avoided speaking opportunities—I spent over 30 years of my life being scared of speaking. That was until I decided to do something about it. Through that journey of finding ways to get comfortable speaking to groups, I learned from some amazing professional speakers. In this book, I'll share those lessons with you.

We often compare ourselves to others we perceive to be much better at speaking and think we can't get anywhere near as good as they are. What we fail to appreciate is that they have probably put in a lot of effort behind the scenes, but we don't see all that—no one really talks about these things. Everyone has to start somewhere—there is no such thing as an *overnight success*. Presenters are made, not born. Yet, in my experience, I have seen so many people edit themselves out of leadership opportunities because they feel they can't present well.

There is no point in comparing your blooper reel to someone else's show reel. If there is any comparison that is useful to make, it's this one: Have you improved incrementally since yesterday? The only benchmark is your own. I do think it's important to watch and learn from great communicators and leaders, but in an inspirational way. I'll share what I think are good examples with you throughout this book.

Confidence is something you build—there is no magic wand.

Some of the thoughts that go through our minds are linked to concerns about getting it right:

- What if I forget what to say and my mind goes blank?
- What if my slides don't work?
- They will be critical and judge me.
- What if I get a question I can't handle? I'll look stupid…

We get what we focus on. It depends on how much weight we give to self-talk.

My first international speaking opportunity was derailed before I had started. I had been invited to speak to a group of regional managers of a European media organization. All of the thoughts listed above were going through my mind, but I told myself to rely on my hours of preparation and trust that everything would be okay. I was taking my own laptop with the slide deck loaded onto it. I didn't make it any more complicated than that—no video clips or use of audio requiring speakers. I had made sure that there would be a screen in the conference room and someone would be there to help me set up. I got to the venue an hour early, so that I could set up in the room before the delegates arrived. Small problem. The owners of the company were in that room having a meeting—I couldn't get in there. In fact, I didn't get in there until my presentation was due to start—I walked in with all the delegates. The IT guy came in, hooked up my laptop to a TV screen and left, never to be seen again. Well, in theory, what could go wrong?

This meeting space was state of the art—floor to ceiling windows on all sides, with an amazing view of a harbor down below. Everything was designed to a high specification, except the setup was not great for my presentation. There was only a tiny glass coffee table, which was a foot high from the floor, and there were about 30 people in a room that could only comfortably hold 20, theatre style. Imagine this—a four-feet deep space for me to move around in at the front of the room and my laptop basically sitting on the floor with no easy way to see my screen. I hadn't practiced for this! Anyway, the adrenaline is going and already I notice this is a tough crowd. People are checking e-mails on their electronic devices. After a pleasant introduction from my host, I started with my opening. Just then, I noticed from the corner of my eye that the screen had gone blank and for a split second I panicked—I was looking at a 90-minute segment without visual aids if I didn't sort something out. The IT guy was nowhere near, and no one in the audience offered assistance. I made some comment about relying on technology (the irony of saying this to a media company) and checked the cable connecting my laptop to the TV. I realized that as the cable was too short to reach this tiny table, so it was stretched too much and the connection just needed pushing in. Hurrah, the screen came back on again and I was able to carry on.

Things like that are not a big deal in and of themselves, but if we interpret them as disasters and they affect our mindset, then it can be bad. Thoughts of failing and looking unprofessional went through my mind at the same time as trying to locate the problem and not turn my back on the audience who clearly had better things to do with their phones. I was used to having AV support when I had spoken before, so I hadn't planned for having to solve my own problem in this way.

The two things I took away from that day were that you always have a choice about how to direct your mindset. You can let something like that eat away at you and zap your energy because it didn't go perfectly or you acknowledge it and move on. I survived that experience and managed to turn round a disengaged audience, which was a huge confidence boost. The second take away for me was that you can never be overprepared. Back then, I didn't have a back up of my talk in the form of handouts or similar, but now I have a plan B—if the slides don't work, I might use a flip chart or introduce more audience interaction. I make sure I can always carry on.

What makes a good presentation then?

In this book, I have referred to other speakers to help you see and hear what they do that works. I have relied mainly on talks hosted on the TED.com platform, as these videos are in the public domain and will be around for a long time for us to enjoy. You should be able to link to them easily.

Remember this—presentations are an investment of time for both presenter and the audience. Time is money. I don't say that in a cynical way, but in business, it is true.

Even if you are presenting to colleagues in the same building as you, they will have spent time getting to and from the presentation room and then will sit through the meeting or presentation in which you are delivering content. The travel time increases, of course, when external visitors attend. While they are in the room with you, they are not being productive.

The one question that goes through their minds is *what's in it for me?* They want to know if you are worth their time. You definitely don't want to waste their time—the key is in finding the balance between content and the time you are speaking for.

Your Intention

Whenever anyone gives a presentation or delivers a speech, there has to be a reason for doing so. What is your intention or reason? No technique will be enough to compensate for a lack of purpose or enthusiasm on your part. It could just be that you have been asked to give a presentation or it is a requirement in a job interview. What else? What do you want to get out of the presentation?

We are all in the business of selling—either our services or products or ideas. We live in a very competitive world, and pitching for work or contracts is much more common these days. You may not be a professional salesperson, but are a professional who has to sell. That's why, investing time in working on your presentation skills is important.

What outcome do you want from your presentation? Is it:

- New clients
- Networking with potential clients
- Increased profile
- More confidence
- Adding value to your audience by helping them learn something new or do their jobs better

Whether it's generating leads, pitching to new clients, delivering training, reporting to the board, or whatever is important for you in your role, give it some serious thought. It's important to get clear about what you want to achieve, as it sets the tone for your entire presentation—both content and delivery.

If you only take away one thing from this book, I hope it's this: put yourself in their shoes. If you put your focus on the audience experience, then the quality and impact of your presentation will increase.

Most of us dread the thought of sitting through boring and pointless presentations. This book covers many suggestions on how to improve your presentations and serve your audience better.

Presentations in Other Forms

As a manager and leader, you will have many responsibilities and get involved with a number of different situations. Your role may require you to:

- Chair meetings
- Conduct training sessions or workshops
- Brief team members
- Report to board members or managers
- Attend interviews
- Provide feedback to junior team members
- Conduct appraisals
- Pitch presentations
- Introduce a speaker at a seminar or conference

While the main focus of this book is designing and delivering a presentation in the form of a talk or speech, most of the ideas and techniques are just as useful for the situations we just considered.

CHAPTER 1

Your Audience

When getting up to deliver a presentation, most people never stop to consider what is going on in the minds of the audience. Who are you speaking to and what do *they* want?

> The fundamental question you need to answer is:
> "What is in it for me?"

If you are reading this book, your presentations will most likely be delivered in your workplace and your audience will probably be your colleagues. They may, however, also be other stakeholders, such as clients, potential clients, or even prospective employers, if you have to give a presentation at an interview.

Background Research

It might seem obvious, but it is important to know who is going to be in the room.

If it's an external audience, you won't know that much about them. They may be invited guests such as clients or suppliers, or you may be going elsewhere to present, for example, at an industry conference or convention. It is, however, possible to get to know your audience better.

These days, there is no excuse for not finding out information relating to audience members. The Internet is a fantastic resource. Start by looking at their company website or social media profile such as www.linkedin.com, which is probably most relevant for business information.

What about information you already hold on your client relationship management (CRM) platform? If you send out newsletters or host seminars, then you already have data that could help you. It depends on what exactly you collect, of course, but some systems can be really sophisticated. You can log basic details on your CRM, such as name and job title, but you might also log what newsletters they have signed up to and what seminars they have attended at your offices in the past. At a firm where I used to work, we could log every client interaction we ever had. At a glance, we could see which colleagues had met with that client and what intelligence they had gathered. Most of this information was used by our marketing and business development teams, but looking at this type of data can also give you clues about someone's interests and help you to tailor your presentation accordingly.

Then, there is the direct approach to finding out what matters to your audience. You could just ask them by giving them a call to find out what they want to get out of the presentation. You only want to give them what they are most interested in—not everything that you may know on the topic. Each individual member will have a different perspective.

If you are presenting to a senior team or board of directors you don't know so well, talk to a few people at that level to find out what works for them. If it's a team you manage or other internal colleagues, you may already be familiar with the personalities and their level of existing knowledge. Use that as a basis for tailoring your talk.

- Do they want detail or an overview?
- Are there specific issues they want you to address?
- What ideas or skills do they want to retain from your presentation?
- What are their job titles or roles? What do they do on a daily basis?
- What are the current hot topics in this industry?
- How many will be in the audience?
- What is the age group?
- Are there industry-specific terms or jargon you need to be familiar with?
- Are they willing to participate and get involved or just want to listen?

This will help you decide whether to incorporate activities.

Put yourself in their shoes. Begin to see things through the eyes of others.

Other ways in which you can research what they may be interested in are through:

- Industry newsletters
- Relevant websites that may be of interest to them
- Social media posts such as trending topics on Twitter
- Podcast shows in related subject areas

Do not skip this important fact-finding step.

Audience Objective

Unless you know what the audience is interested in, you are probably going to disappoint them in some way. Their objective will be different from your own objective. Understanding your audience and industry before you speak is crucial. What do they need to hear and experience in order for you to persuade them?

Have you ever walked out of a presentation and thought, "I didn't actually hear anything I don't already know" or worse, "I didn't understand what that was all about!" Quite often, the audience's needs are not met because they were never identified in the first place. Do your homework. It will pay dividends.

Your audience wants to be informed and entertained. You will, no doubt, have heard the phrase "people like to do business with people they know, like, and trust." We buy from people when we feel they "get" us, when we feel understood. Solving a problem only gets us so far, as does having a great reputation for being an expert at something. It's not enough just being good at what you do.

In this digital age we live in, we need to give more value. People have short attention spans and can get pretty much anything they want or find out most things via the Internet. There are many things competing for their time.

Going to a meeting or seminar better be worth their time. Think about what they will find interesting and compelling. What key information do they need to take away with them in order to implement changes? Is it clear enough so that there is no room for misunderstanding? What do they already know and how can you build on that to share something of value that will gain their interest?

When you tap into the conversation in your audience's heads and respond to that, you can be more persuasive. You want them to feel as if you have prepared something just for them, rather than adopting a cookie-cutter approach.

If you had to sum up in one sentence, how would you describe the objective or goal of your presentation?

It is useful to remember that we each have our own unique way of seeing the world and processing information based on our attitudes and beliefs. This means that something may seem completely obvious to you, but the other person just doesn't get it. For example, some people like a lot of technical information or detailed facts, while others only want the headlines. When you structure your content, you need to balance these competing needs, which we will look at in more detail later.

There will be times when you have to cover challenging ground. When you have an opinion about something, there will be members of your audience who are quite likely to have a different view—a critical audience. You need to bear this in mind when researching your audience, designing your content, and adopting the right mindset during your presentation. Your duty is to serve the audience by giving them value.

Other aspects to consider regarding your audience and where they are coming from are:

- Not everyone in the room wants to be there—they may have been told to attend by their manager
- There may be pressures in the business such as a restructure, jobs being laid off
- Some people, for example, more experienced colleagues, may have more knowledge than you

There can be a lot to think about in order to give the best value and serve the majority of the audience when you have different agendas to balance. The starting point is to find out what these agendas are through your research.

Putting the audience at the heart of your presentation is key to making the content or message relevant, but it's you who brings it to life. The speakers who make an impact are those who present their own views. It might be tempting to hone your content to make sure it pleases everyone and offends or challenges no one, but then, what is the point of you presenting the material? Your opinion is part of the value you bring to the table.

Key Points

- Research company websites and social media profiles to find out areas of interest for your target audience.
- Ask an audience member directly what they want to get out of the presentation
- Think about their motivation for being there.
- Ask yourself: Is what you are intending to share going to be worth their time?

Links

www.linkedin.com

CHAPTER 2

Structure and Planning

Once you have identified the needs of your audience, it is time to create your content. It is important to have high-quality content that is relevant to your audience—whether it provides a solution to a problem or informs them of the next steps.

Do not go to your presentation software yet—whether that is Power-Point, Keynote, or something else. I would suggest that it is too soon to use these tools.

The mistake that a lot of people make in their approach to presentations is to think of a topic, settle upon a title, and then go straight into writing the content within PowerPoint or similar software. Programs like these lead to linear thinking—producing one slide after another using the standard bullet point templates.

The problem with this is that it is easy to slip into report writing mode. Presentations are not written reports. We don't speak how we write. Written text comes across as more formal and less warm than your spoken voice.

Let's take a look at this in terms of movies. When books are adapted into movies, screenwriters rework the text to make it work for the screen—from 2D to 3D. That is how you want to think about presentations.

There are a few instances when people do need to read when presenting. I once helped an art historian prepare for her presentation at The Royal Academy of Arts in London. She told me that reading her paper out loud was the expected format, but she wanted to make the experience the best it could be. Obviously, there were many restrictions she had to comply with, so we worked on her tonality and voice projection—things that were within the parameters of what was allowed.

Start with the End

Begin with the end in mind. If you imagine taking your audience on a trip, what is the destination or end point? It is so important to get clear about this before you really get into the planning of your material.

In his greatly acclaimed book on personal leadership, *The 7 Habits of Highly Effective People*, Stephen R. Covey talks about how powerful it is to begin with the end point in mind. In the book, Habit 2 is about applying principles of personal leadership to many different circumstances. It means starting with a clear understanding of your destination. If you know where you are heading, then you can reverse-engineer the process and work out where you want to begin.

Think about it in terms of project management and logistics. The end goal would be to provide a product or service to clients or stakeholders. When you know the result you need to deliver, you can work backward to assess what needs to be put in place to deliver on time and within budget. Crafting your presentation is no different.

How would you end this statement? "By the end of my presentation, the audience will…"

Your end point could be:

- A feeling—are you going to inspire them?
- Change of some sort—for example, behavior, way of working or practice
- Taking action—asking them to do something

Once you know what you want to leave the audience with, you can plot the route of how you can get them there. Having a blueprint or road-map will help you get organized and give you a framework that you can use for any type of presentation.

Timeline

When will you get it done by? We are all busy people with constant demands on our time, so finding more time to prepare for a presentation is quite a challenge. I find it helps to block out time in my calendar at regular intervals, so I have a designated slot to just focus on my presentation. I switch off my phone and e-mail during that time. The only things you can manage are your priorities. Put it on your calendar. Plan for your preparation by blocking out time. It might not be easy to fit into your normal busy workday and may involve some out-of-office hours. Otherwise, life just gets in the way.

Brainstorming

Brainstorming helps you become more engaged with your material and goal. A great way to start is by sketching out ideas on a blank sheet of paper. Create a mind map or spider diagram. This is a visual way of organizing your ideas.

Mind maps were made popular by author Tony Buzan (http://www.tonybuzan.com). If you want to go digital, free and paid apps are available in the Google and Apple stores, for example, that you can download and try for yourself.

Start with a blank sheet of paper or screen and then build on the main idea. Put your main topic in the middle and then branch off your key points off that. (See the example below)

The first time you do this, just get all ideas and thoughts down. Brain dump of all the possible material related to your talk. You can later edit or remove anything not useful. It can be quite difficult to do this at first because you will be tempted to edit and dismiss ideas before even writing them down. That refining comes later.

The advantage of going for quantity over quality at this stage is to find content that resonates with your audience. Collecting as many ideas as possible puts you in a better position to do that. If you edit yourself too soon, the tendency is to create content that you want to share and not what your audience needs.

You do not have to do this in one sitting—it may actually take several days to come up with all your ideas—but by doing it this way, you capture them on one sheet of paper, which you will clean up later.

Once you have gone through the first round of brainstorming, leave your map to one side and come back to it later. This gives your unconscious mind a chance to process the material.

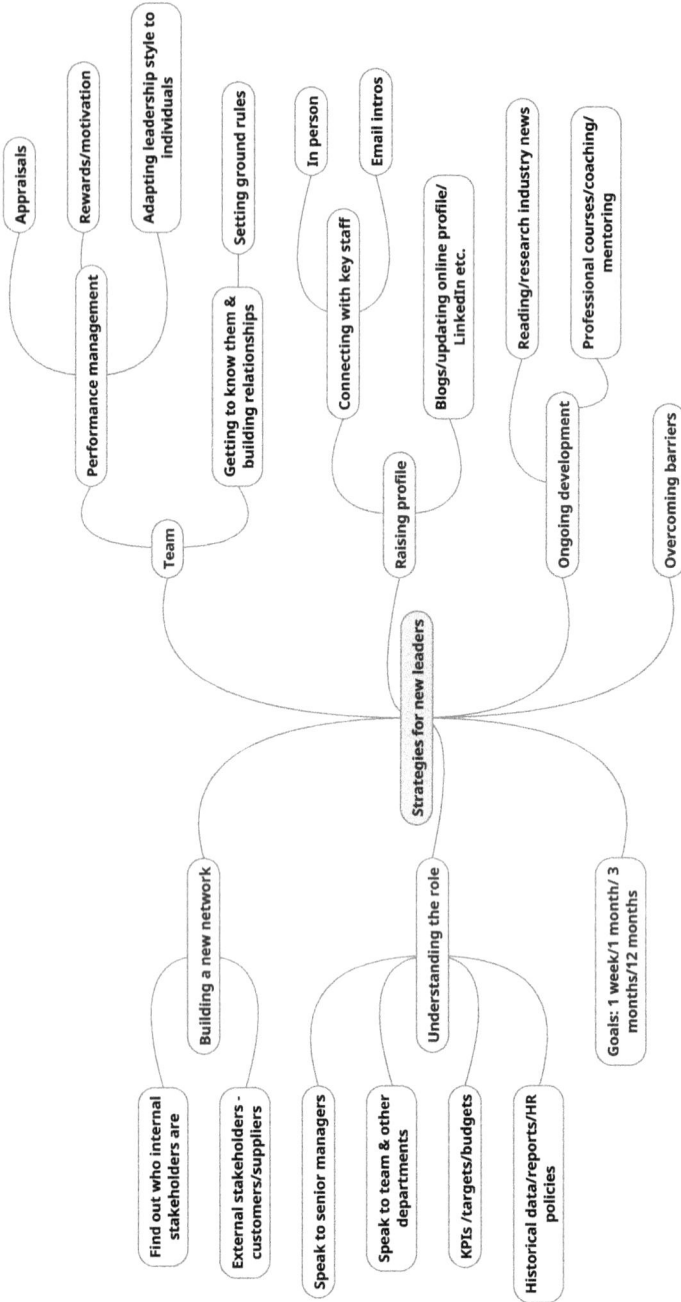

Strategies for new leaders

- **Team**
  - Performance management
    - Appraisals
    - Rewards/motivation
    - Adapting leadership style to individuals
  - Getting to know them & building relationships
    - Setting ground rules
- Raising profile
  - Connecting with key staff
    - In person
    - Email intros
  - Blogs/updating online profile/ LinkedIn etc.
- Ongoing development
  - Reading/research industry news
  - Professional courses/coaching/ mentoring
- Overcoming barriers
- Building a new network
  - Find out who internal stakeholders are
  - External stakeholders - customers/suppliers
- Understanding the role
  - Speak to senior managers
  - Speak to team & other departments
  - KPIs /targets/budgets
  - Historical data/reports/HR policies
- Goals: 1 week/1 month/ 3 months/12 months

You might also want to show your mind map to colleagues for their input. This is also a great tool for workshops and problem solving.

Mind Palace or Memory Palace

This is a memory technique that associates physical locations with thoughts we want to memorize. The physical locations are used as memory pegs that we hang our thoughts on—we visually associate what we want to remember with a well-known physical location.

How to see the world as Sherlock Holmes does:

Sherlock Holmes is a fictional character created by Sir Arthur Conan Doyle in Victorian England in the late 19th century. He solves crimes and brilliantly outsmarts everyone with his incredible attention to detail—he sees things that others miss. The character and the crime stories created by Conan Doyle have stood the test of time and still have worldwide appeal. Since 2010, the BBC channel has been producing a show starring Benedict Cumberbatch as Sherlock and Martin Freeman as Dr. Watson, with audiences waiting impatiently every year for the release of a new series.

What enables Sherlock to show his brilliance and solve crimes is a combination of his superhuman observation technique and the ability to link his findings to information stored from past experience—information that had been filed away in his mind palace. He knows exactly how to recall information when he needs it, and he chooses what goes in there in the first place. Most of us do not think consciously about how we go about storing data.

There are many books based on Sherlock Holmes and his mind palace. In her book, *Mastermind: How To Think Like Sherlock Holmes,* Maria Konnikova says the space in our head is specially designed for storage. It is a fascinating book exploring how we think and make decisions through the influence of our preferences and bias.

Sherlock himself describes this space as being so crammed full that useful knowledge is crowded out or jumbled, which makes it very difficult to find. A skillful workman is careful as to where he puts information. "I consider that a man's brain originally is like a little empty attic, and you have to stock it with such furniture as you choose" (Sherlock Holmes in *A study In Scarlet*—Sir Arthur Conan Doyle). The furniture he talks about represents our thoughts.

This concept of a mind palace is not new. It is based on our use of spatial memory—inside our home, route to work, and so on. The concept is that our mind organizes material in a certain way. It is a useful technique to improve memory generally, but also for networking and remembering speeches. More on this later.

According to a myth:

A Greek poet, Simonides of Ceos, was at a banquet and escaped death when he stepped out to speak with two young men. He did not find them and the banqueting hall collapsed behind him, crushing the remaining diners to death. Simonides was able to help identify them by remembering where each person had been seated in the hall. This ability to remember on location became known as the method of loci, later used by historic scholars to memorize their speeches.

Our memory and processing can become more efficient if we use it well. For me, personally, I think of my mind as one big filing cabinet where everything is stored in labeled drawers—they have to be put in the right drawer, of course, in order to be found later!

Nowadays, this technique is used by competitors in memory championships worldwide.

How is this relevant to presentations? Sometimes, when you sit down to create content, your mind goes blank and inspiration does not come when you need it. What tends to happen is that, we get useful ideas when we are actually doing something else, such as driving or reading. We fall into this trap of thinking we will remember it later when we go back to our presentation preparation, but in reality, it's gone, probably somewhere in our brain attic, as Sherlock would say, but not pegged into our memory palace yet, so we cannot access it.

I would, therefore, encourage you to find a way to capture ideas and key phrases that come to you in seemingly random moments. We all walk around with mini computers in our pockets in the guise of smartphones. Open up the Notes app and add any ideas you have. Sending an e-mail or text to yourself works too. I listen to a lot of podcasts across many different industries, usually when I am traveling or running. If I can, I will send myself an e-mail with ideas that I want to capture. If I can't do that right away, I'll make sure that as soon as I get to my destination or end of my run, I send that e-mail.

There are also tools such as Evernote (https://evernote.com) that can be really helpful in assisting you with collecting useful information to use later. You can send e-mails to your Evernote account, clip and save articles you are reading online, and much more.

Or, you could just go low tech and keep a small notebook with you that you can use to record your thoughts. Basically, it does not matter what you do, just find a way to get into the habit of capturing information that will help you later.

General Industry Awareness

I think it is good practice to keep up to date with what is going on in your area of business and what is important for your clients. In the Internet age that we live in, it is not too difficult to do a bit of research and find background information for your presentations, so that you can tailor them to your audience.

Whatever industry you work in, there will be numerous blogs, articles, magazines, and podcasts you have access to, such as:

Entrepreneur.com
Businessinsider.com
Forbes.com
HuffingtonPost.co.uk
HBR IdeaCast Podcast https://itunes.apple.com/gb/podcast/hbr-ideacast/id152022135?mt=2 (Harvard Business Review is subscription-only, but the weekly podcast is free.)

These are just some suggestions—for you, personally, there will be more specific sources you can access. You can also look at client websites, news sites, government sites, and so on. Sign up to their newsletters or follow their blogs.

It is fantastic that all of this information is available to us, but on the flip side, it can be overwhelming. You are probably thinking your inbox is the bane of your life already, so why would you sign up for yet more incoming mail? You can bookmark sites in your browser, save e-mails in a specific research folder, or print electronic PDF versions of interesting articles and come back to them when you have the time to read them. It is always a good idea to file some of these things for later, as you never know when it might become useful.

Storyboard

Once you have all the possible ideas in front of you, the process of building your roadmap or blueprint for your talk can begin. Take your ideas from the brainstorming stage and arrange them in some sort of order. Storyboarding is a good technique for planning the order of your content.

A storyboard is a sketch or outline for organizing content in a sequence. It provides a high-level view of your presentation—a framework or skeleton roadmap.

Use individual cards or sticky notes to write your main ideas on and lay them out on a table or put them up on the wall. The great thing about them is that they are moveable, so you can keep organizing until you find the perfect structure. Then, chunk down to work on one section at a time—adding content that supports that segment. Write ideas for images, stories, and facts.

Structure your material like this and you have a skeleton framework that can be ready at short notice. This is a concise representation of your entire talk, which can be shortened or lengthened depending on the scenario.

To explain it another way, your key points are now arranged in the order you will talk about them. It is like a cheat sheet you can carry around with you or keep on your desk. Every so often, prior to your presentation, you can glance at it to become really familiar with the content. It forms your plan with key signposts that you can use to cover a 10-minute slot in a team meeting or extend into a 45-minute keynote. The only difference between the short version and the long version is that you can expand on your points with more examples or stories. We will cover stories in the next chapter.

Using Existing Material

You don't always have to start from the beginning—start collecting any existing material. This can be previous presentations on similar topics, articles, research papers, or anything else related to your topic.

There is not necessarily anything wrong with using previous presentations if the content is still relevant. Check for out-of-date material or concepts and update those. I would still recommend going through the brainstorming phase and looking for other content, so that you can add a fresh look to the existing presentation and hone it to suit the needs of your next audience.

Choose Your Best Points

Now that you have spent time generating ideas, it is time to trim and get your content down to the key points. Like many of us, you will be tempted to want to leave in as much as possible because we fear missing out key information and we think that it adds credibility. You have just invested a lot of time in gathering all this content together, after all. Resist the temptation. You need to prioritize and choose only content that is essential to your core message or key points.

Inexperienced presenters often cram in too much information, usually onto their slide deck. Be ruthless.

Ask yourself this question: "Is all that information relevant and necessary?" Whether you are showcasing your expertise, teaching a new concept, or providing a strategy update, make it relevant.

Remember you are taking your audience from point A to point B. You only need what is absolutely essential to get from A to B. Pick your most impactful points and filter out the rest. Go back to your main message or topic—each piece of content you choose to leave in must support that.

Let's look at this another way. If you don't filter out additional content, you risk making the audience work hard to sift through all your content in order to figure out the important points.

Simple versus simplistic. Great presentations are easy to follow. You might be so familiar with your ideas that even complex points may seem obvious to you. That is not necessarily going to work for someone not involved with the project or content on a daily basis or if they are hearing it for the first time. Trim out everything until you have enough material to support three to five key messages.

We are literally bombarded with millions of bits of information in any given second. This is way too much for our conscious minds to handle. That is why, if you remember back to when you learned to drive a car, it was so overwhelming at first. There were mirrors, pedals, signals plus whatever else was going on outside on the road with other drivers. Over time, by becoming familiar with these processes, our conscious minds no longer need to pay attention because the driving happens on autopilot.

In his book *Flow*, Mihaly Csikszentmihalyi talks about this in some detail. In any given moment, our minds filter out what we do not absolutely need to know in that instance, so we can focus only on what matters there and then. What that means is not everything you say will be picked up by everyone in the room. We filter information by taking in only what is necessary, according to our personal beliefs and attitudes. That is why, we each perceive experiences in a unique way.

For example, when a number of people are exposed to the same event, such as a road accident, witnesses will give differing accounts, because they filter differently.

How does this relate to your content?

Choose a handful of your most important points and build your structure around them. Somewhere between three to five points is about as much as people will remember. We can only hold small amounts of information in our short-term memory.

A few clear points will stand out against a mass of information. Remember if you can take them from A to B successfully without losing them along the way, they will appreciate it. If you blind them with science to show how intelligent you are, then you will lose them. Explain how specifically what you are sharing is applicable to them or their role—no more and no less.

A few years ago, I came across a video that shows this concept incredibly well. It is called the Monkey Business Illusion.

The Monkey Business Illusion video: https://www.youtube.com/watch?v=IGQmdoK_ZfY

The video produced by Daniel Simons has over seven million views. I won't spoil it for you if you have not seen it yet—chances are you have, but if not, I'll put a description of it at the end of this chapter.

What this type of experiment shows is that we focus on different things from those our neighbors pay attention to. Every time I have shown this in a workshop, even people who know to expect the changes miss something else.

Multisensory Language

We experience the world through our five senses:

- Visual—seeing
- Auditory—hearing
- Kinesthetic—feeling
- Olfactory—smelling
- Gustatory—tasting

For example, smell can take us to a specific time in the past. Music can do the same—hook us onto a memory. In addition to our five senses, we use self-talk or logical analysis. We use all of these of course, but generally, people have a preference in the way they like to receive information. Some people think in pictures or images, others in sounds, feelings, or self-talk or logic.

In your audience, you will have people with a mix of preferences. This will influence how you prepare and deliver your presentation. Use a mix of delivery methods, focusing on the four most relevant aspects:

- Visual—like to see pictures, videos, diagrams
- Auditory—like to listen and tune into the tone of voice
- Kinesthetic—have a feeling for things and want to experience things through physical activities
- Self-talk—they want facts and data

You can choose words to connect with people's preferences as well:

Auditory = hear, sound, listen, tune in, ring, resonate
Visual = see, look, picture, perspective, crystal clear, observe
Kinesthetic = feel, touch, catch, grasp, concrete, handle

Neutral words for those that are analytical = think, know, interesting, experience, logical, concept

To read more about how we use our senses in perceiving the world around us in context of the workplace, take a look at *NLP at work (Neurolinguistic Programming)* by Sue Knight.

Vivid language and description make content more memorable than a vague overview. Our world is multidimensional. Understanding this concept of selective filtering is not just useful in crafting presentations, but is also valuable when managing people.

In any given moment, we experience many million bits of information—too much for us to consciously cope with. We, therefore, have to filter out most of what we are exposed to in order to focus on what matters to us in that moment. Pause for a moment to think about what your left shoe feels like on your foot. Until you put your attention to it, you were not aware of it because it was not necessary to know.

We each filter this vast amount of information in unique ways. You and I will focus on slightly different aspects of this sea of information coming at us. We each make sense of our experiences according to our model of the world—which includes our beliefs and values.

Early on in my legal career, I handled personal injury cases on behalf of large insurance companies. In order to defend these cases, we had to investigate. Part of the investigation was to interview witnesses. Almost every single time, all the witnesses gave slightly different accounts. They had all witnessed the same event, so why the variance? They all perceived the same incident through their own filters, according to their personal filters.

You want your content to be sharp and relevant—there is no room for padding. Keeping your outline simple and clean will create a better impact than a rambling narrative that is aimless. This is not the same as simplistic, which is dumbing down.

Anatomy of a Presentation

Think about dividing up your framework into the following three main sections:

Why

This is the most critical part. This is where you show the audience you care about their issue or problem. The reason why they want to know about what you are sharing. This is why, it is worth paying attention. Remember, it is the audience's perspective—their *why*, not yours. Whet their appetite—this is where you sell your idea and awaken curiosity.

Imagine they will most likely be thinking "Why should I sit here and listen to you?" or "What's in it for me?"

Answering their "why" is how you want to start.

What

This is content that includes fact and logic and probably the area you are most familiar with, and this is usually where most average speakers spend the majority of their time and quite often skip the preceding "why" section. This is, of course, an important section, but until you have got buy-in, it will not have as much impact.

How

In this part, you show them how what you have shared affects them— how it might help them, using the information you just gave them.

When ordering your content, start with the "why," move into the "what," and then explain the "how." You have completed the most time-consuming phase, now that you have gone through the structuring part.

Now that you have this basic roadmap, you can go back and start to add material that will enhance your message and make it more memorable, such as examples, stories, and interaction.

Open and Close

Once you have your three to five key points, you want to build your opening and closing comments. The middle part of the presentation is the easiest to formulate. The beginning and end may take more work.

Your opening needs to set the scene and grab attention right away. Get this bit wrong and you lose the audience. You want to capture their attention early. If you have it from the start, it will be easier to hold on to it throughout your presentation. If you do not grab it at the beginning, you will have to work harder to get it.

Think about how you want to make your first impression. How are you going to hook them in? Create curiosity, describe a benefit, make a promise?

Memorize that opening—one of the rare times, I would recommend memorizing content word for word.

Do not fall into the trap of opening by telling the audience your company is the best in the industry for a particular product or service, with numerous employees all over the world or something similar. How uninspiring is that? This is a common mistake that people make because they think it will build credibility by putting credentials in the opening. There are better ways to showcase expertise and team capability.

Remember, your audience most likely will not care about these things. They are thinking "WIIFM!" (What's in it for me). The way to grab their attention is to make it relevant to them—their issues, problems, or areas of interest. This ties in with the "why" section we looked at earlier.

Stay away from uninspiring "me-focused" opening lines when introducing yourself:

"Hello …my name is…thank you for inviting me to speak…"

"It's good to see so many of you here today…"

"Thank you for coming to my presentation today, I hope you find it useful…"

"Let me tell about our company…"

If you want to share information about yourself at the start, give someone else your introduction, so that it does not come across as self-promotion. This lets you get straight into providing value. You could write your own introduction—that makes it easy for hosts sometimes, as they often struggle with finding interesting things to say. Some points you may want to include in your introduction:

- Why are you qualified to speak on this topic?
- What are the relevant achievements, academic or otherwise?
- Who have you helped?

Part of my introduction is the fact that I had a fear of speaking for a long time before finding a way through that and now truly believe anyone can speak. The audience can relate to that.

You are building credibility, but also need to answer WIIFM. Consider these aspects:

- What will they learn?
- Does it save them money or make more?
- Make life easier?

Your opening should be confident and engaging, providing the audience with an assurance you are worth their time, otherwise they will tune out. The first few seconds are when you grab their attention.

Craft something jargon free. Create a hook that captures their attention and links to your main points. The opening needs to highlight the direction in which the presentation will go. Say something that will make them sit up and take notice. Try one of the following techniques in your opening:

- Pose a thought-provoking question—one that sparks interest, making them curious. This can be rhetorical or asking for audience participation with a show of hands.
- Ask them to "Imagine if…"
- Start with a shocking or interesting fact.
- Use a quote—choose one that fits in with your theme and has not been overused.
- Start with a story.
- Use humor—you can bring this in with an amusing story or a joke, but this takes a lot of practice and testing and you want it to be great; otherwise, it can fall flat.

You can use the same ideas listed here to finish your talk. Whichever technique you use, link it to what you want the audience to do or think. The ending needs to bring everything together and tie in with both your intention and the objectives for the audience. It is important that this part of your presentation is memorable.

Your closing remark needs to be even more powerful than your opening—it will be the thing they are most likely to remember as it is the most recent.

In the same way as opening with "thank you for inviting me…" is not very powerful, ending in a similar way is not impactful. You can still be respectful and thank the audience and host for inviting you or listening, but you also need to leave them with an impact by using something like:

- A call to action
- Asking for the contract or sale

Not every presentation has to have a call to action. Other ways in which you can end:

- A quote
- Summary of your main points

Introducing a Speaker

The main focus of this book so far has been about you as the presenter. You may, at some point, be in the role of a host, chairing a conference or event. In such cases, you will be conducting the introductions.

Introducing another speaker is a skill. It is a kind of presentation. It sets the scene for the speech, creates the first impression, and builds audience anticipation. If possible, find out in advance if the speaker has written an introduction or wants you to cover certain points. If you can, do some research before the event and write something. If it is not possible to do that, for example, if you are asked at the last minute to do the introductions, sketch it out on a piece of paper before you get onto your feet. Use what you can—something about the speaker and some key points from their topic.

"My impression of this person is…what they are about to share will… please welcome…"

The Monkey Business Illusion Part 2

Following on from the previous video link, here is the background. The scenario is that two teams are passing a basketball between them. People watching the video are asked to count how many times the ball is passed between the players in the white shirts. But, that is not the only thing going on. A gorilla walks into the game, stops and beats his chest, then leaves. The curtain in the background changes color and one person on the team wearing black shirts leaves the screen. Most people are so focused on counting the ball passes that they just do not see the gorilla come into the game, and if they see him or know about him already, they do not see the other changes that are also happening. Very interesting experiment.

Key Points

- Start with the end in mind and reverse-engineer your content.
- Set aside time in your calendar to work on your presentation; otherwise, it doesn't happen.
- Use mind mapping to brainstorm your raw data without editing, then leave it for a few days.
- Research industry websites and blogs to find useful material to build into your content.
- Use multisensory material and language to appeal to all sectors of the audience.
- Choose three to five main points only and keep it simple.
- Use the *Why, What, How* format to order your content.
- Craft a strong opening that answers WIIFM.
- End with a clear message—what do you want the audience to do or think?

Links

Evernote
https://evernote.com
Useful Business Websites
Entrepreneur.com
Businessinsider.com

Forbes.com
HuffingtonPost.co.uk
Harvard Business Review weekly podcast—hbr-ideacast:
https://itunes.apple.com/gb/podcast/hbr-ideacast/id152022135?mt=2
The Monkey Business Illusion
www.youtube.com/watch?v=IGQmdoK_ZfY

Books

Covey, S.R. 2004. *The 7 Habits of Highly Effective People*. New York, NY: Simon and Schuster.

Konnikova, M. 2013. *Mastermind: How To Think Like Sherlock Holmes*. Edinburgh, UK: Canongate Books Ltd.

Csikszentmihalyi, M. 2008. *Flow*. Harper Perennial Modern Classics.

Knight, S. 2009. *NLP at work*. Nicholas Brearly Publishing.

CHAPTER 3

Stories, Metaphors, and Anecdotes

You will spend a lot of time working on your content, ensuring it's relevant and accurate. Once you have gone through the brainstorming and structuring phases, you want to look at how to bring the material to life and make it memorable. Add some color and contrast.

People won't remember the details, but will remember the stories. Create a memorable moment that people will talk about for a long time afterward.

> *"I've learned that people will forget what you said, people will forget what you did, but people will never forget how you made them feel…"*
> —Maya Angelou

I was sitting in the audience a few years ago at a lecture given by a professor of a well-known business school in the United Kingdom. The lecture was about the power of storytelling. He shared with us how people come up to him all the time and say, "I still remember that story you told…" The professor told us "what is remarkable about that is *I* don't remember when I told that story or where I was but they do!" By the way, this professor has been voted the best teacher twice in recent years by his students. That has to be because he makes his content relevant and interesting for his students, right?

We all know friends and family who are good storytellers. When they share stories around the dinner table or over drinks, we remember them for years afterward. We love to hear them—even when we have heard the same story many times, we encourage the storyteller to share it with someone new because we want them to hear it too.

A key skill great speakers have is storytelling. The use of stories and analogies is critical to being a good communicator. There is nothing more powerful than an engaging story that captures attention. Telling stories forces you to get away from your slide deck and focus on connection with your audience.

We have been learning through stories since time began. As children, we grew up with them. Storytelling facilitates problem solving, as we each individually see images in our minds and join up the dots according to our values and beliefs. If you think about it, human beings have been passing on knowledge from generation to generation through stories such as folklore and religious texts—long before slides were ever invented.

Can you remember at least five presentations that you sat through over the last few years? I challenge you to remember the key points. You would be doing well if you can remember what the speaker shared and the ideas you took away with you. If you do remember anything, was it because the point was made using a story or anecdote? You know from personal experience that our memory fades as time passes—within a few days of attending a presentation, people will retain just a fraction of the information shared, and this becomes less as time moves on. Anecdotes and storytelling hook the audience into your message and take them on a journey, drawing people in. Think about how the advertising industry does this.

Build your point into a story so that it not only makes it memorable, but also reinforces it. Make your content stick by incorporating your learning points or message into a story.

If you're thinking I can never come up with stories for work-related topics, don't worry. Stories are typically normal personal everyday accounts. This is how we, in the audience, can relate to what you are sharing because we can connect with the material at an emotional level. Stories allow us to associate with the underlying message in our own way—we create our own mind movies.

Facts tell. Emotions sell.

What about if you are thinking, my content doesn't lend itself to a story? I believe that every topic can be associated with a story to help the audience really "get" the point you want to make. Even if you can't come up with a story that is a case in point, there will be some story material that you can use to enhance your message. I will give you some examples of speakers who demonstrate how possible this really is.

TED talks are fantastic to watch and learn from, particularly to see and hear how speakers use storytelling. These talks are publicly available on the TED.com website and are short bite-sized presentations less than 18 minutes long on any topic you might care to know about. It is an amazing resource for managers.

Sir Ken Robinson is a British creativity expert with a wry sense of humor. His TED video "Do Schools Kill Creativity" has been viewed over 40 million times since 2006. If you haven't already seen it, it's definitely worth a look, www.ted.com/talks/ken_robinson_says_schools_kill_creativity.

Ken's presentation is packed full of stories and jokes. What I want to impress upon you is that what he is saying and the way in which is he saying it is not beyond your reach. Ken fluctuates between humor and serious points. If you watch closely, he tells a story and then ties it into a point he wants to make—sign-posting it for us and making it sticky at the same time. Then, it's rinse and repeat—the same format throughout.

Let's consider two stories, which appear in the initial five minutes of the video. The first story he tells is not his own and is very short. He describes a scene between a little girl and her teacher. The little girl is drawing a picture and so the teacher asks her what she is drawing.

"I'm drawing God."

The teacher says, "but we don't know what God looks like," to which the girl replies, "you will in a minute!"

That's it, short and sweet. It took hardly any time to tell it and the audience laughed. Easy payoff. Why this is such a great example for storytelling is that it's not a personal story. Ken tells us he heard it recently— we don't know where or when. It doesn't matter. You can do this as well. Think of all the stories you hear from other people or the ones you read about in the news or on blogs. Use them and credit the source if you can. Just don't pass it off as your own.

The second story Ken shares is personal—about his four-year-old son taking part in a nativity play. His son played one of the three wise men. He and the other two boys playing wise men, wearing tea towels on their heads, were bringing gifts of gold, frankincense, and myrrh. One of them messed up his line a bit. Again, there is laughter from the audience. This is just an everyday occurrence that most people in the audience can easily relate to. We may not all have children, but we have all been children at that age in similar scenarios.

So, what does Ken do with these seemingly unremarkable stories? The theme that he pulls us back to is that kids will take a chance and are not frightened of being wrong, but by the time they grow up, they lose this ability. This is how he ties in the entertaining short stories with his serious message of "Do Schools Kill Creativity." In this TED talk, we can all relate to the two school scenarios and make the connection.

You can achieve this effect as well—it just takes proper preparation. The stories you share do not need to be very long—somewhere around one to three minutes is about right, just like the two aforementioned examples.

Vignettes or Mini Speeches

You want to start building a bank of stories in the same way in which you collect ideas before the brainstorming phase. Once you have a story idea, you can develop it. To develop your story, write it out in full script, including any dialog. Then, leave it for a few days. When you come back to it, you can start to trim all the extra words that really don't add anything or are not necessary to get you to the punchline. Like a well-crafted joke that has a setup, then punchline structure, your setup is the scene in the story and your punchline is the payoff at the end of the story. When Ken Robinson talks about the little girl drawing God, there is very little scene-building needed before the payoff when the girl says "You will in a minute!"

When creating your stories, you'll go through several steps. The first one is like a brain dump—resist the urge to edit and leave it for a few days. When you come back to it, you can start to refine it. It's like you're writing a joke. Your aim is to get to the punchline as quickly and efficiently as possible—paint the picture in as few words as possible. Design your story so that you begin telling it from the point of action—like in Hollywood. It is much more powerful to start the action and then build in any relevant background afterward.

Just like structuring your content, think about what your end point, punchline, or message will be. This will help you reverse engineer the setup.

This process does take time, but every time you edit your story, it gets stronger. Keep refining like this for a few drafts—at least three. When you are happy with the final version, you have a ready-to-go story that can slot into any future presentation or speaking opportunity.

These short story segments are called vignettes. A vignette is a mini story—making a point in story form. Just like a joke, the payoff justifies the timeline—you want to get there in the most efficient way possible without any fluff. A payoff is like the punchline. In a story, you may have many payoffs along the way.

Over time, you will build a catalog of vignettes that you can use again and again. That is where efficiency in early preparation pays off—you do not need to reinvent the wheel every time you are asked to speak. Each one stands alone. You prepare and test them individually.

The beauty of refining your vignettes in this way is that you rehearse your story so many times that you know it unconsciously and can call it up at a moment's notice without having to start from scratch—learn once, use it many times. You can then connect them in any order you want, to fit your topic and length of presentation.

If you have never used stories, start small—just work in one example for your next presentation, and gradually, over time, build from there. It gets better with practice and experience.

We tell stories all the time anyway. Think about the conversations you have over coffee or a drink—everyday examples of real-life experiences that are either your own or some else's.

Dialog

Dialog within your stories will bring them to life and draw the audience in.

Another way to introduce this is to use self-talk. Thinking out loud has the same effect. The dialog takes the story from past tense and brings it into the present—involving the audience even more, inviting them in.

It is more elegant and more effective than narrating "she said…"

If you can, give your character a distinct voice. If you do that, you won't need to give a physical description.

In August 2016, Darren Tay, a young lawyer from Singapore, became the world champion of public speaking at the annual Toastmasters International Speech Contest. After being introduced by the host (contest chair), Darren walks onto the stage and pauses for effect. Then, when he does speak, it is in the voice of one of the characters in the story. The premise of Darren's speech is being bullied at school. He takes us through his experiences at the hands of the school bully, and he gives the bully a speaking part in his story. Right from the start, he has the audience on the edge of their seats, capturing their interest.

The topic is serious and can make people uncomfortable. By being playful and using stories, Darren makes the audience not only feel comfortable, but draws them into the scene.

By the way, he also uses a prop. The prop is a pair of white underpants that he pulls on over his suit. As you can imagine, he gets a few laughs at this point. We will come back to this prop later when we talk about visuals in Chapter 5.

Watch his opening line (video hosted on the Toastmasters YouTube channel www.youtube.com/watch?v=v26CcifgEq4). His words are not his own. He opens with a dialog—the voice of the bully. Like the opening sequence in a gripping movie or first few lines of a great novel, he takes us straight into the action.

The other thing you notice is that Darren actually uses several short scenes in just over seven minutes. They are mini anecdotes cleverly honed over months of writing, editing, and testing in front of live audiences, which are then sewn together around the core message he shares.

Watch the full seven-minute speech here, as reported by Business Insider:

http://uk.businessinsider.com/toastmasters-public-speaking-champion-darren-tay-2016-8/?r=US&IR=T/#-1

Story Format

Premise is what the story is about—the theme. A typical story format is the hero's journey. You know the one where the hero has to save the city and faces his nemesis in a long hard-fought battle along the way, but triumphs in the end. At the core of a story like this, there is usually a conflict or challenge—something at stake.

The hero's journey is not the only way to share a story. You can approach it from a personal angle—something that you overcame and can inspire others to do as well: "…That was hard for me once and I found a way through it." Sharing facts like this help us make a connection with the audience. This probably makes most of you uncomfortable—the idea of being vulnerable or transparent about such things. It isn't a weakness—it's what makes us relatable. This is also a good way to inspire and share lessons with team members and people you manage or mentor.

You can get more ideas from history and speeches that left an imprint on our world. *Speeches That Changed The World* (Simon Sebag Montefiore—Quercus Publishing, 2010) features famous speeches by Martin Luther King, President Kennedy, Nelson Mandela, and many more. This book gives us fantastic insights on the structure of great stories—ones that move people to think or do something different.

When you put it all together and find a place to slot your story into your content framework, don't say "I'm going to tell you a story…" just get into it with a natural segue way. A good example is when Ken says, "when my son was 4…"

Tell it in the present tense—like it is happening now, so that the scene can unfold right there in front of them.

Case Studies

How can you do this with one of your stories? Imagine you are sharing a client case study. What was the problem? What was the turning point? Set the scene of the current reality, creating tension. Then, contrast that with what could be. The gap between the two is how you guide your audience to a different way of thinking. Your hero could be a client or customer with a problem—talk about a clear lesson of coming out the other side. Set the scene and give some background, rather than just sharing the basic facts. Talk about the type of company, the challenge, and so on.

Or, you could use testimonials in the form of written quotes for your slide deck or as video clips. Make sure that they show how you specifically helped the client or how the client benefited from your service or product.

Borrowing Stories

As with Ken's TED talk, stories you share don't have to be from your personal experience. You can borrow them. Sporting achievements past or present are a great source of material for topics such as achieving goals, team work, leadership, and inspiration, generally. Talking about leadership theories and styles can be quite boring. It makes it much more interesting to give some background in a story or share some history.

Consider the following two examples of borrowed stories that I often use when teaching or speaking about management and leadership topics:

The Hawthorne Effect

Elton Mayo was a professor of industrial research at Harvard University in the 1920s. He carried out workplace behavioral research at the Western Electric Company's Hawthorne Plant in Cicero, Chicago. During the study, 20,000 workers were observed over a period of 10 years. The initial experiment looked at whether improved lighting would have an effect on motivation and productivity, which it did. What was interesting was that productivity also increased for the control group for whom conditions remained unchanged. The only aspect for the control group that had been varied was the fact that they were informed they would be part of the study.

What these experiments showed was that, people are mainly motivated by emotional factors, such as a feeling of being involved or receiving attention, and not merely by improved workplace conditions or economic factors.

President Kennedy's Visit

On a visit to the U.S. NASA Space Center in 1961, President Kennedy apparently asked a janitor who was cleaning the floor nearby "what's your job here?"

"Well Mr. President, I'm helping to put a man on the moon."

This is a good story to refer to when talking about understanding the vision of an organization and the desire of individuals to be part of something bigger than themselves.

It may be that these stories have been used many times and everyone knows them. But, you get the idea.

Prepare your story based on your audience, framing it in the context of their challenges. When people can identify themselves through their jobs or lives as part of the story, you are more likely to get their attention. Your story needs to have a structure built around a point you want to illustrate—just like Ken Robinson demonstrates.

Metaphors and Analogies

Very often, concepts and ideas that are difficult to grasp are easier to understand if explained by way of metaphors or analogies. For example, getting used to adopting all the techniques in this book is like learning to drive a car. The first time you got into the driver's seat, there were so many things to think about. Now, however, you can drive effortlessly without consciously thinking about all the individual elements. Getting comfortable with new presentation techniques becomes second nature in time, just like driving.

> Analogies and metaphors are both figures of speech in which reference is made to one thing in order to explain another. They are used as tools of comparison to help us understand things better.

Analogies compare things, so we can see the relationship between them—comparing one thing and another to highlight the similarity. Metaphors compare an existing thing to another unrelated object or situation. It can be a word or phrase used as a comparison. Unlike an analogy that is used to highlight the similarity between two things, metaphors are unrelated and can even be contradictory.

It is not important to know the definitions of these devices of analogies or metaphors—what is important is to use them in ways that describe things that make sense for your audience. It all comes down to making comparisons that help your point stick.

Here are some examples to get you thinking:

From the world of literature, William Shakespeare, *As You Like It*:

"All the world's a stage, and all the men and women merely players..." comparing life with a play.

In his book, *Men Are From Mars And Women Are From Venus*, author John Gray (an expert in communication and relationships) compares men and women to species from totally different planets—hence, the constant miscommunication. If you haven't come across this book yet, it is worth checking out—John uses lots of amusing examples of how men and women are at cross purposes all the time—from keeping score to going into the man cave.

One of the more well-known examples I often use when talking about time management is the rocks in a bucket example. You have four items that represent the tasks or priorities in your life, and the challenge is to get them all into a bucket. The bucket represents the time you have and the four items are big rocks, gravel, sand, and water.

Steven Covey mentions it in his book *First Things First* (Simon and Schuster 1994). The big rocks are a metaphor for the important tasks in our life (work or outside). The gravel, sand, and water are less crucial and interrupt us from things that ought to be a priority. If you put the big rocks into the bucket first, everything else fits in around it, but if you do it in any other order you risk missing out on important things.

These types of examples help us reframe a problem or situation with a new perspective, making the strange familiar.

Example of phrases we use all the time in our everyday language are:

Marathon not a sprint
Score a touchdown
Batting for the same team
Time is money
Cross fertilization
Well-oiled machine
Ride out the storm
Blueprint or roadmap
Tailored or bespoke
Foundation = strength
Climbing the career ladder
Make lemonade out of lemons

Zero sum game—if I win, you lose

Cutting out dead wood—become more efficient

Opening gambit or end game—comparison to moves in a chess game

Weakest link—the chain is only as strong as its weakest link

Think outside the box—think differently

Show the ropes or run a tight ship or plot a course—sailing phrases

What goes through your mind as you read these words: "…A long stemmed glass filled halfway with wine…"

What kind of glass did you picture? Was the wine red or white? Was your glass half empty or half full? There specific points are missing from the sentence, but your mind fills in the gaps effortlessly. That is the power of using devices such as analogies, metaphors, anecdotes, and stories—your audience can make sense of what you share in their own way with their individual filters according to their model of the world.

Compare your concept to something that the audience can relate to or understand to give them a reference point. It helps us create a shortcut in our minds.

Key Points

- Remember that we all learn through stories.
- Start collecting everyday stories from your life.
- Keep stories to one to three minutes.
- Watch TED videos for inspiration and technique.
- Write the story in full and then edit after several days.
- Prepare the story once and use forever.
- Use dialog for your characters to draw in the audience.
- Borrow stories from history or sports.
- Use analogies to compare something complex to something the audience can relate to.

Links

TED

TED.com

Ken Robinson: Do Schools Kill Creativity
www.ted.com/talks/ken_robinson_says_schools_kill_creativity
Darren Tay Toastmaster Winning Speech—excerpt
www.youtube.com/watch?v=v26CcifgEq4
Darren Tay full video within Business Insider article
http://uk.businessinsider.com/toastmasters-public-speaking-champion-darren-
tay-2016-8/?r=US&IR=T/#-1

Books

Montefiore, S.S. 2010. *Speeches That Changed The World*. London, UK: Quercus
Publishing.
Gray, J. 1999. *Men Are From Mars And Women Are From Venus*. Vermillion.
Covey, S.R., A.R. Merrill, and R.R. Merrill. 1994. *First Things First*. New York,
NY: Simon and Schuster.

CHAPTER 4

Data and Context

Putting facts and figures into context is very important. Time and again, we see figures used in presentations, sometimes quite large numbers, without any reference to what the relevance is. The numbers are presented on a chart in very tiny text font that hardly anyone can read. In business, we refer to concepts such as key performance indicators, sales figures, market share, and so on all the time.

> Data means nothing without context. Put it next to a concrete example to help others see what you are talking about. Think about using analogies.

Numbers feature in every industry sector and within departments or teams within those sectors. We live in a digital age—technology is everywhere. If you live and breathe technical ideas and information, you need to find a way to explain it in everyday language.

Figures should be used to illustrate or prove the point you make. The problem is that, too often, financial information in presentations shows up as one slide of complex figures after another.

A lot of people make the mistake of thinking that stacking their presentation content with data makes the message more credible or persuasive. Actually, it just confuses the listener. You, as the speaker, may well be the expert compared to the audience you are speaking to. Focus on the data your audience cares about the most and make it easy for them to understand. Let's look at a very simple example.

Say you are making a point about gender diversity in the boardroom and that only 20 percent of the board members are women, a quick comparison for your audience would be:

"That's like saying just the front row in this room represents the percentage of women in the boardroom."

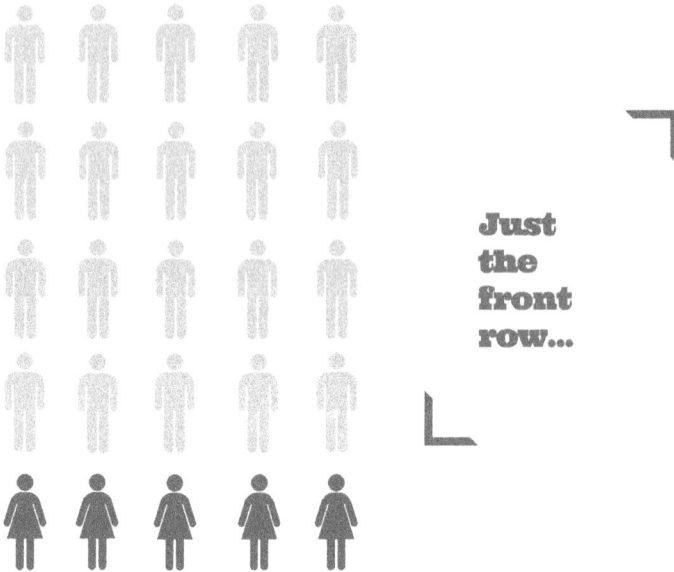

Just
the
front
row...

Put it next to something they understand. What does this mean for you?

If you talk about market share, put it up against competitors in a bar or pie chart. Just talking in terms of percentages is useful, but we really get it when you put the number next to that of a competitor—it is more visual and memorable.

Flow charts and infographics are really useful in making dry data more visual. Consider the following examples:

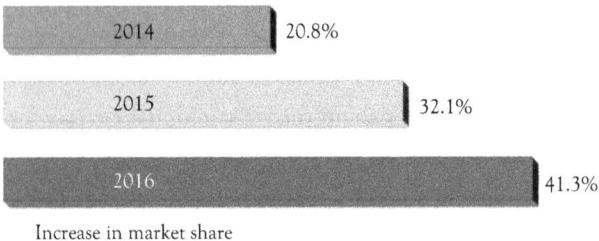

2014	20.8%
2015	32.1%
2016	41.3%

Increase in market share

This type of bar chart is simple to create. Click on "insert shape" and then select "format shape" to change the colors and add a three-dimensional (3D) effect.

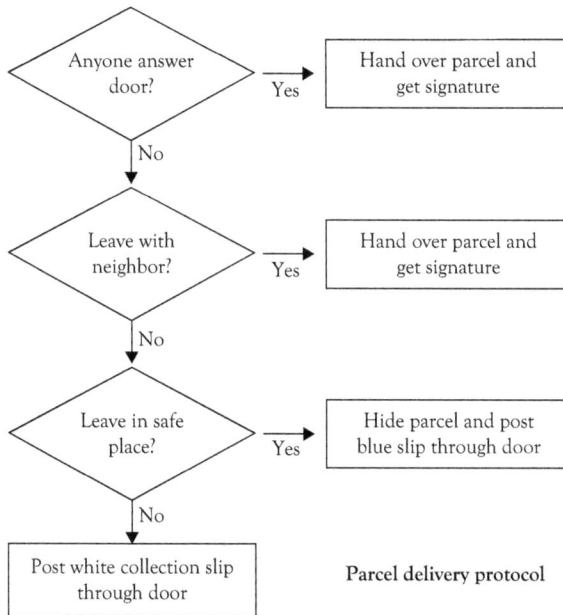

Parcel delivery protocol

Parcel Delivery Protocol

- Anyone answer the door? Yes = hand over and get signature. No = possibly leave with neighbor
- Leave with neighbor? Yes = hand over parcel and get signature. No = possibly leave in safe place
- Leave in safe place? Yes = post blue slip through door. No = post white collection slip through door

The preceding flow chart is cleaner and much more interesting than the uninspiring bullet-point slide. This type of effect is easy to create within PowerPoint itself using the flowchart drop-down menu or adding in shapes and lines.

A good resource for creating info graphics is Canva (there are both free and paid versions): www.canva.com.

Whatever you may think about Steve Jobs as a boss or entrepreneur, whether you are an Apple fan or not, one thing that most of us agree on is that he was great at putting ideas into context. Apple doesn't sell computers. They sell an experience. Often referred to as the greatest corporate speaker ever, Steve Jobs put numbers and technical data into context incredibly well.

Every time Apple launched a new product, Jobs would practice for hours—he was a perfectionist. He rehearsed until he got it right, then made it look effortless. He improved over the years.

When the MacBook Air Notebook was launched, he stood on the stage and then pulled this incredibly thin notebook out of an office manila envelope and said: "This is the new MacBook Air and you can get a feel for how thin it is." He could have just told us it was the world's thinnest notebook—all the stats were there for the people who love techy information to note what the dimensions were. Yet, by putting the notebook next to or inside an everyday object, we really get to see how thin this device really is. We have a tangible reference point and don't just need to take his word for it or try to make sense of the dimensions.

Steve Jobs Jan 2008 MacBook Air Video—the relevant part is at about 52 minutes:

www.youtube.com/watch?v=1CgAKBf4bbU

He adopted the same technique with the launch of the Apple iPod years before—1,000 songs in your pocket. The size of a deck of cards.

iPod is the size of a deck of cards – 1000 songs in your pocket

Another great example of putting technical data into context is Jill Bolt Taylor's TED talk, which has been viewed over 19 million times. Jill is a scientist who studies the brain. She had the unique opportunity to study the functionality of the brain through first-hand experience when she suffered a major stroke. She tells us the story of how she lived through it, stage by stage.

As with Ken Robinson, whom we looked at earlier in chapter 3 on storytelling, Jill has a very conversational speaking style. Her slides are simple, and there are not many of them. Her opening slide shows a photo with her brother to set the scene as to why she decided to get into her field of expertise—her brother has schizophrenia.

Then we get the prop. Unexpectedly, she brings a human brain onto the stage so that we can all see exactly what the two hemispheres of our brains look like. It's a sight you don't forget in a while—a powerful hook. The key point here is the way in which she puts scientific information into context for us in the audience. She makes the complex simple. Her language is simple and easy to follow, yet, in no way does she patronize the audience. It's all about context—we can see, feel, and hear what she went through because Jill describes it so well.

When you watch the video, you will see that, for the most part, Jill speaks as if she is talking to a friend—this is not a performance in a theatre. You can explain complicated data and tell stories in this way too.

Jill Bolte Taylor: My Stroke of Insight

www.ted.com/talks/jill_bolte_taylor_s_powerful_stroke_of_insight

Start thinking outside the box if you have data you want to include. Whatever it is, there has to be a way to put it next to everyday examples. Find fun facts and link to those.

I recently worked with a manager from the food and drinks sector. The focus of the talk was about reducing waste. One of the items was milk. He opened with: "How many gallons would it take to fill an Olympic size pool? That is the volume we are wasting right now." Powerful imagery, right?

You might be worried that the main focus of your presentation needs to be complex financial data. Not necessarily. Pick your main points and put some context around it in the way we just looked at, then hold the rest back—more details can be sent later in a handout. If you hand out any printed material with figures on during your presentation, you need to give your audience time to read it.

The key message here is keep it simple and resist overwhelming the audience—it will make more impact.

Key Points

- Put your data next to an everyday object that the audience knows and can relate to.
- Use flow charts and infographics to show data in a visual way.
- Hold back on detailed data and put it into a handout for later distribution.
- Keep it simple—don't overwhelm the audience with too much data.

Links

Steve Jobs Jan 2008 MacBook Air Video—the relevant part is at about 52 minutes:
www.youtube.com/watch?v=1CgAKBf4bbU
Jill Bolte Taylor: My Stroke of Insight
www.ted.com/talks/jill_bolte_taylor_s_powerful_stroke_of_insight
Canva
www.canva.com

CHAPTER 5

Designing Slides and Visual Aids

A picture can paint a thousand words. Using good-quality visuals can be a very powerful way to enhance your message and make it more memorable. Research shows that retention of information increases when information is shared both visually and orally.

Visual aids give your audience:

- Something to look at—very important especially for those who prefer to receive information visually
- A means of putting your message into context, especially if it is complex, by providing an illustration or example to show exactly what you mean
- Variety—another source of stimulation

Start with a framework for your deck—a sketch to scope out what slides you want to support each point or story you want to highlight, such as the storyboard technique we looked at for arranging your key points. When you have an idea about the order and concept for each slide, then you can source images, charts, and so on.

Slide Decks

Your slides could be your visual element, but not necessarily. They are your support act—slides don't give the presentation, *you* do. Only after you have organized your content, refined your points, and developed your stories are you ready to add visuals in the form of slides. People don't come to view your slideshow; they come to hear and see you. Many presenters use slides as a crutch. Of course, slides are an important part of many business presentations, but too much emphasis is placed on them, rather than the message itself.

Quite often senior executives and managers will ask assistants or even a design company to prepare the slide deck for them as it seems like a better use of time. That's real life. However, this section goes into a lot of detail about how to produce great visuals so that you can direct an assistant to create something that reflects you best. Ideally, as you are the speaker, it works better if you produce your own slides, especially if you are not familiar with the slide software.

Knowing how it all works at least gives you the confidence under pressure when for some reason something fails to work on the actual day. Get to know how it all works and what you like before you outsource anything. If you are getting help with your slide deck, send a copy of your mind map or sketch out the outline of the slides you need to your assistant or design team.

There is a presumption that using slides makes the presentation look more professional. However, the reality is that improper use of slides can make your presentation look bad. Poorly designed slides can bring down the tone of your presentation in many ways:

- Densely populated slides with lots of text
- Distorted images that are too fuzzy to see
- Lots of data and graphs that are difficult to read
- Bad choice of animation or too much of it

We all know the phrase "death by PowerPoint." This is what the audience experiences when faced with endless slides crammed with text.

What are members of the audience thinking when this happens?

- Try to read the text on the slide
- Concentrate on what the speaker is saying
- Just give up and start looking at their phone because you lost them

In his book, *Presentation Zen*, Garr Reynolds calls this type of presentation "slideuments"—a mash up of slides and documents. Resist the urge to cram in too much. This is not ideal. Too often, we see this kind of deck—possibly due to last-minute preparation when the speaker hasn't made time to refine the content.

Not only is too much text a problem for the audience, it also can be a distraction for the speaker as she or he gets drawn into reading his or her own slides, rather than looking at the audience. A lot of people don't realize this is happening until it is pointed out to them. Mediocre speakers use slides as a teleprompter and a crutch. The slides are there for your audience and not as a script for you.

Many business presenters approach designing slides in this way. I often sit on a judging panel for start-ups competing to secure a place in an accelerator program in which they will receive mentoring and support with resources. Those that are successful eventually become ready for investment. When those start-up companies pitch to investors, they'll put together a slide deck to support their presentation.

Here's the interesting thing about the way in which they prepare them. Potential investors like to see the slide deck in advance. In order for the slides to make any sense for someone just reading the deck in isolation without the entrepreneur being present, there has to be some text added in. However, for the face-to-face meeting, that text is not there. The versions are "read deck" and "slide deck." Read deck is for reading. Slide deck is for presenting.

Only use tools such as slides if they enhance understanding. This goes for physical handouts too. Don't let materials become the focus.

If you have a slide up on a screen, you are drawing the attention of your audience to the screen, and every time you change the slide, the same thing happens. Add to this situation that most seminar or conference rooms have projection screens positioned in the center of the room so that you, the presenter, have to stand in a corner to one side to let the audience read what is on the screen. If you put less text on your slides you don't have to keep adjusting your delivery to allow for the content to be read.

Getting the Most from PowerPoint

People use PowerPoint like they are driving a Ferrari at 20 miles per hour simply because they don't know just how much is possible. It is an amazing piece of software that will help you design beautiful slides that improve the audience experience. The same is true for Keynote or similar, of course. Unfortunately, a lot of slide presentations are full of bullet-point text. It doesn't help that when you open PowerPoint, the default is a bullet template. Sometimes, text is necessary and can be helpful, but large unbroken slabs of text on a slide will turn people off.

If you do decide to use words, restrict your content to three lines per slide and give your audience time to read them. Create space between lines. Think simple and clean—very few words per slide. Too many words on the slides will overload their brains and make them work harder. Keep to one idea per slide.

Blanking Your Screen

Never leave slides up on the screen if they are not related to what you are talking about. This only distracts the audience. Instead click on "B" on your keyboard to turn the screen black or "W" to turn it white. When you are ready to get back into the slides, press the same key again.

Hide Slides

Sometimes, you want to skip slides. You may have been asked to cut your time short. Alternatively, you are using the same slideshow for different clients, and there are one or two slides that are only relevant to the respective clients. You can hide those slides by selecting the slideshow option on your toolbar and then scrolling down to "hide slide" and selecting that.

Slide Transitions and Animation

My personal preference is not to use any fancy slide transitions—things such as the slide bouncing into the next frame or blowing up in a puff of smoke. But, it's a matter of personal choice. I would say, it is more professional to click on the next slide without any fancy tricks, as that can distract from your message.

The same advice goes for animation—for example, when you bring one paragraph at a time in sequence. It can be useful to do this, but just be careful about what affects you apply to each click of your mouse. If you do choose to use special effects such as having your paragraph come flying in from one side of the screen, then be consistent and use the same effect for all the moving parts so that it appears more fluid.

Font

Style of font is another consideration. This is a matter of personal choice again. Think about the audience and the image you want to portray. Your organization may be conservative or very laid back. You might want to pick something that reflects the culture, and of course, you as the presenter. Whatever you go for, pick something that pops out from the big screen and is easy to read from the back of the room.

To keep your slides simple and effective, stick to no more than two different styles. Any more than that and your visuals start to look disorganized. You want to aim for a smooth consistent look throughout your presentation. Once you have created them, go back and check whether you have the same look and feel running through each one—check for style and size. Font size ideally needs to be a minimum of point 28 to stand out on a big screen. Choose fonts that are easy to read, such as such as Arial or Helvetica, so that the person in the back row can read it. The goal is to produce something that is consistent and professional.

Contrast and Text Color

Small font is not the only problem, though. Choice of color for both font and background will have an impact on the audience experience. If there is not enough contrast for the text to stand out, then it will be difficult to read once the slides are projected onto the big screen. If you have corporate colors, choose something sympathetic to your branding, but keep your focus on the audience experience.

What looks good at your desk is not necessarily what works in the presentation space, as the lighting in the room will have an impact. If the room is bright, use dark font on a light background. If the room is dark, you can use light font on a dark background. The only way to know if your slides will be visible to the person in the back row is to test them either in the actual presentation room or somewhere similar.

Images

It is not that difficult to create visually appealing slides. Replace your text with stunning images. Our minds can process images much faster than reading words. A well-chosen picture leaves things open to interpretation.

With less content on your slide, you are free to talk about your subject without being restrained by a script. You know what to say about that image or point, and because you don't have too many words on the screen you are not tied to a script word for word. Every time you present on the same topic, you will deliver it in a different way anyway, and with this setup, your audience will never know.

What sort of images should you use? Ask yourself whether you can connect it to the point you are making. Photos work at an emotional level. Use them to set the scene to a story. Graphics and charts can also work well if there is very little text on them.

Use large, high-quality pictures. One beautiful photo can be incredibly compelling. When you insert them, use full bleed—that means fill the entire screen with that image, no headings or branding. If you want to put a few words over it, use a text box, but keep the words to a minimum. Take a look at the following example:

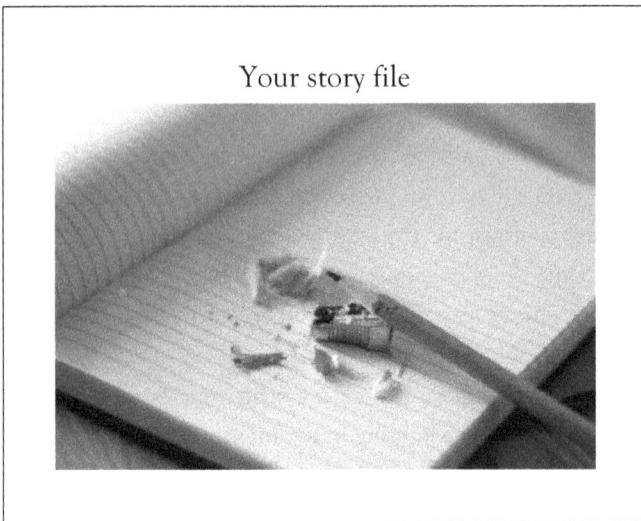

This is how most presenters insert pictures into a slide using the normal default slide format with a heading.

This is the same picture as in the preceding slide, but expanded out to cover the entire slide. No heading needed. If you want to add words, select "insert text box," type your text, and place it over your image. Much more professional-looking and appealing.

You can find text boxes under the "insert" option on your main toolbar at the top. Once you select the text box option, PowerPoint positions your keyboard cursor onto your chosen slide—just start typing something straight into it; otherwise, if you click away, it can look as if your text box has disappeared. You can then format the size, font, and color by highlighting your text and selecting "format" on the main toolbar at the top.

Shapes, Flowcharts, and Graphs

How many times have you sat in an audience and the speaker has a graph on the screen with lots of labels and data that are just too tiny to read, then she or he says something like "you probably can't read this at the back but..." Replacing bullet points with a visual chart is much more appealing for your audience and easier to understand. Using shapes, such as Venn diagrams, pie charts, and simple bar charts help to illustrate complex concepts. Such visual elements help to put data such as statistics and trends into context.

For example, rather than listing figures related to profit or loss or sales per quarter as bullet points, represent them in a bar chart. Keep the graph simple and clutter-free, so that it can be seen clearly. This includes labels on the axes. You can bring in parts of the graph gradually as you talk about each section. This is not too difficult when you know how to use the features of PowerPoint shapes and graphs. However, a really easy way to create the same effect is to have a number of slides gradually adding an extra section each time. As you click through, it will create the same effect as if you had animation of several moving parts on one slide.

Using flowcharts is another great way to display relationships and progression. For example, if you are explaining a sequence of processes or timelines, a flowchart is much more appealing than a list of bullet points. You could provide a summary of the key points, for example, within a flow diagram, like the example shown earlier in Chapter 4:

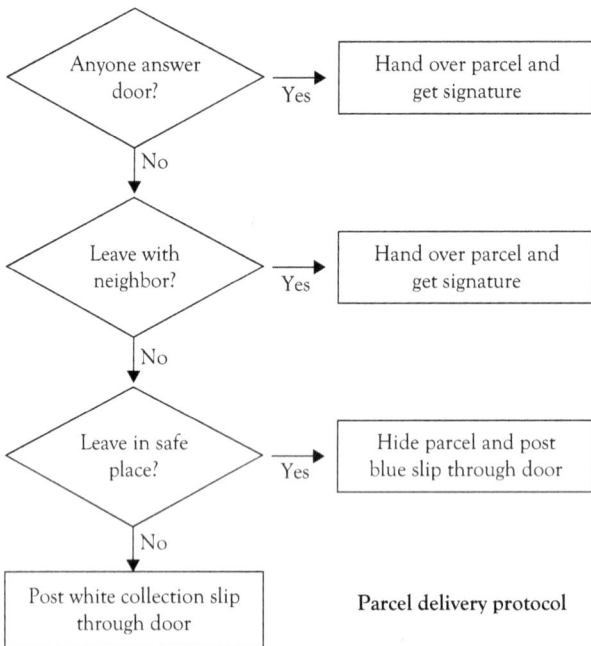

Parcel delivery protocol

An info graphic with text is much more visual than text alone. Sites such as Canva.com are great resources for creating info graphics such as the example that follows. You can also use the shapes within PowerPoint to create these if you have the time and imagination to play around with the options.

THE

BEST TIMES

TO POST ON

SOCIAL MEDIA

FACEBOOK

Thursday & Friday
1:00-3:00pm

INSTAGRAM

Monday
3:00-4:00pm

PINTEREST

Saturday
8:00-11:00pm

TWITTER

Monday-Friday
12:00-6:00pm

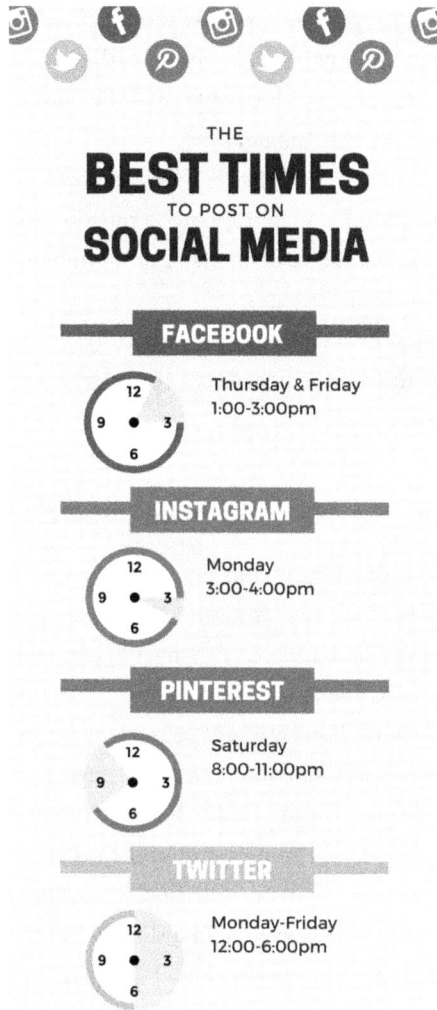

This infographic has been created using a template in Canva.

Resources for Images and Copyright

A word of caution regarding copyright of images and video clips: using images found through well-known search engines on the Internet usually will require obtaining permission. This should be obvious if you see a watermark or copyright symbol stamped on the picture. Some people take no notice of this and use them anyway—the faint watermark on the slide is a giveaway and says "amateur."

There are, however, plenty of sites where you can download "royalty free" images (sites giving you appropriate permission to use the images). Some offer the images at no cost; others have varying prices ranging from single purchases to annual licenses.

The other option is to take your own photos.

At the end of this chapter, there is a list of sites where you can find royalty-free images.

Grouping Images, Shapes, and So On

This is such an amazing option and not many people know about it or use it. It is one of the best ways you can ensure that any moving parts on your slide do not get knocked out of whack when you send them over to someone who has a different version of PowerPoint that is not entirely compatible with yours. For example, you might be using a flow chart to demonstrate a process—all your boxes are lined up with connecting arrows and text sitting on top of each box describing what each phase represents. To lock them all into one image, click on "edit" and "select all" capturing all the moving parts, then find "group" under the "arrange" button on your toolbar. This may be in a slightly different place on your version of PowerPoint, for example, under "format" or "drawing tools," but it will be there somewhere.

Here is link from Microsoft Support demonstrating visually how to do this:

https://support.office.com/en-GB/article/Group-or-ungroup-shapes-pictures-or-other-objects-a7374c35-20fe-4e0a-9637-7de7d844724b

Video and Audio

You can use video clips embedded into your slides if they support your message. Using video clips can be useful for getting your point across in a more meaningful way and can help create an emotional connection to your message. Videos can be especially useful for demonstrating a technique or process. They are also a great way to include testimonials. Make sure your clip is not too long—remember people have short attention spans.

Similarly, music can help connect with people's emotions. You might be thinking it is not appropriate in a business setting. Not necessarily. Music can create a range of emotions and alter attitudes. Think about songs that make you feel happy. If you are referring to a specific time period or era, then choosing a recognizable piece of music will transport the audience to that place.

One of the many challenges speakers have with using PowerPoint to create slides is that there are many versions of it. Your version of Power-Point may be different from others, and the options on the menu bar or functions may well be different. Microsoft offers a suite of tutorials for more detailed guidance on all the suggestions I've made earlier.

Here is the link for online PowerPoint training:

https://support.office.com/en-gb/article/PowerPoint-training-40e8c930-cb0b-40d8-82c4-bd53d3398787?ui=en-US&rs=en-GB&ad=GB

Every single item within your slides—whether it is the heading, background, text, or images—can be formatted or designed to your taste. Your imagination is the limit.

Flip Charts and Whiteboards

When you have a small group, slides may be overkill or not appropriate. The audience may benefit from a more interactive format. Flip charts or whiteboards are a great way to go. They are low tech, portable, and do not require much advance preparation.

They work well for getting feedback and generating ideas through brainstorming in an informal way. I actually use them in addition to slides when I am facilitating a training session.

When I say they require very little advance preparation, compared to slides, they do. You still need to think about how you want to use flip charts to demonstrate a point by drawing a chart or listing ideas. When it comes to preparing for drawing difficult graphics, have it done beforehand on a sheet behind the front of the pad.

You can write some of the ideas or key words you want to refer to in your presentation ahead of time. That way you do not have to spend too much time turned away from the audience or worry about messy handwriting while you are talking. To add emphasis as you later go through your prepared flip sheet, you can draw boxes around key words. The other way to prepare is to write or draw guidelines for what you later want to share in faint pencil—especially if it's a chart or diagram. Have enough markers that work—this seems obvious, but is so easy to forget.

If you have a room full of people, you may not want to use this format for your visuals if it is going to be difficult for people at the back of the room to see.

People like to use slides to support their presentations because they can be printed as handouts or e-mailed as an attachment later. Flip chart paper is obviously too large to scan or copy, but you can take photos on your smartphone and circulate that later. I use this technique all the time when facilitating workshops. This works well when breakout groups brainstorm discussion points on a sheet of flip chart paper. Take a photo of each group's idea sheet and circulate it later.

Much of what has been said already can be applied to whiteboards in terms of use of pens and demonstrating in front of small groups. You can't of course tear off sheets of paper and stick them up, but you can wipe that board. Again, if there are key ideas you want to circulate later, take a photo before you wipe the board clean. Many whiteboards are now interactive smart boards—remember the pens are different for them!

Props

This is the three-dimensional (3D) visual aid. Not many people use props, which is a shame. Clever use of props can help your audience remember key concepts and will make your presentation stand out. Of course, if you have a physical product to sell or showcase, then it seems obvious to use that as a prop. However, props don't just need to be limited to products.

Some ideas for you:

- Gold fish bowl filled with dirty water to demonstrate pollution
- Medical experts using skeletons, models of the brain, and so on
- A book the speaker has written or recommends

Remember earlier in Chapter 3 we talked about the white underpants Darren Tay pulled on over his business suit during his winning speech at the Toastmasters World Championships? Props can be used to add humor or introduce variety. Your imagination is the limit.

Darren Tay Toastmaster Winning Speech—excerpt www.youtube. com/watch?v=v26CcifgEq4

Handouts

Bear in mind that anything you pass around or leave on chairs for people to refer to could be a distraction. They can be useful as a visual aid to help explain a complex point or process. Tables and charts are sometimes better printed in hard copy than crammed onto a slide.

I do think it isn't helpful to print your slides three to a page. If you have designed your presentation well, the slides don't mean anything without you anyway, plus they are so small they are not that useful. There is more on this point in Chapter 10.

Interaction with Your Audience

Most of us would agree that an interactive presentation incorporating questions or discussions is engaging. There are ways we can make presentations more fun for the audience. Remember they want to be informed and entertained. If you involve them, they are more likely to remember more.

> Take your audience from passively absorbing your content to wanting to implement your ideas. Turn your presentations into conversations.

We have talked about many different ways in which to keep your audience engaged—through designing content to answering their "why," making slides visually appealing and using stories. We will also look at adding humor in Chapter 7. Another way to involve your audience is by leveraging the slide presentation through technology.

There was a time when it was deemed to be incredibly rude if someone got her or his phone out during your presentation. We've now come full circle and actually want people to share our content live on social media. For example, conferences encourage people to use specific hashtags.

There are many products that are inexpensive or have free versions with enough functionality to let you use polls that the audience can engage with using their smartphones. Unlike asking people to put their hands up and speak out, this works incredibly well. They can answer anonymously and then see how they did compared to the rest of the audience.

The audience can also ask their own questions that you can see come in live and then choose which ones to answer. What's great about these software solutions is that it makes it easy for anyone who is not so confident to speak up by typing a question they really want the answer to. Everyone signed into the link can see other questions listed and can "up vote" the ones they like.

You can even incorporate live tweeting. This raises your profile, creates engagement, and helps connect anyone who couldn't make it to the presentation. Sli.do.com and Glisser.com are just two companies that offer interactive presentation software, and there are many more if you search.

You can add fun elements by incorporating quizzes based around your topic—use the poll functions mentioned earlier to get live results or simply create slides with your questions on them and ask the audience to shout out answers. If you have data to share or results from research studies, get the audience to guess the answers before you reveal them.

The advantage of using some of these interactive presentation tools is that all responses to the questions are stored, so you can use that data later, for example, if you were conducting a poll regarding issues that mattered to your target audience. After your event, you could export the poll results into an infographic and send it to participants as a follow up. There are many more useful functions such as sharing your slides in real time with audience members on their smartphones. Take a look at the links that follow to find out more.

Key Points

- Use high-quality images to fill the screen, rather than text.
- Keep to one idea per slide.
- Choose font size and style that are easy to read from the back of the room.

- Use flow charts instead of bullet points.
- Group your images so that they stay in place.
- Involve your audience through live polls or quizzes.

Links

Glisser
https://glisser.com
Sli.do
https://www.sli.do
Microsoft Support demonstrating grouping visuals:
https://support.office.com/en-GB/article/Group-or-ungroup-shapes-pictures-or-
    other-objects-a7374c35-20fe-4e0a-9637-7de7d844724b
Microsoft PowerPoint Training:
https://support.office.com/en-gb/article/PowerPoint-training-40e8c930-cb0b-
    40d8-82c4-bd53d3398787?ui=en-US&rs=en-GB&ad=GB

Books

Reynolds, G. 2012. *Presentation Zen.* New Riders.
Resources for images:
www.freedigitalphotos.net
www.gettyimages.co.uk
www.gettyimages.com
www.canva.com
www.presentermedia.com
https://stocksnap.io

CHAPTER 6

Delivery

How you say something counts for a lot more than you may imagine. That includes your body movement, use of stage, and your voice. Your communication needs to be congruent—in other words, your delivery needs to match your words. When you are enthusiastic about something, you are better at presenting it.

My recommendation for you is to find your way of being yourself in front of an audience. What does that mean exactly? I like to think of it as "what you see is what you get." The way you are at the front of the room is the way you are in normal everyday conversation without a formal speaker persona to hide behind.

Authenticity

Connecting with the audience is crucial. The starting point is being authentic—show up as who you really are, rather than some detached robot. If you think back to some of the presentations or seminars you have attended, how many times did the speaker look as if he or she had a different persona?

Your style is unique. If you have watched the two TED talks mentioned in previous chapters (Ken Robinson and Jill Bolte Taylor), you saw two very different speaking styles, and yet, both are engaging and effective. In each case, we feel like we know the speaker.

It is your personality that others want to see, not some detached "speaker" persona. People do business with those who they know, like, and trust. Your authenticity is what will resonate with people and make them want to buy into your ideas.

Imagine having a conversation with someone over coffee. That's the level of connection to aim for in your presentation—one conversation at a time. That doesn't mean you can't still be professional.

Smiling is a simple way to build a connection. A genuine smile shows your authenticity. Do not underestimate the power of a smile. It can be so easy to come across as very serious and unapproachable without realizing it, especially if there are some nerves about giving the presentation. A simple smile and relaxing the facial muscles could be as much as you are prepared to do in terms of body language, but it will make a big difference. It puts the audience at ease, too.

Are you simply informing by just delivering information? If you can convey your subject matter in a human and emotional way, people will buy into your idea and you. Many business presenters talk at us as if they were lecturing. But, with a little effort and the right intention, it could be so much different. It is possible to inform and entertain at the same time.

You may not be giving the message for the first time, but remember, for the audience, it is the first time they are hearing it from you.

The 7 Percent to 38 Percent to 55 Percent Communication Rule Misrepresented

It is often said that, in any communication, only 7 percent of the meaning is attached to the words we say—words alone don't have as much impact. This has been misinterpreted. You may recognize the following chart, from articles or workshops on communication.

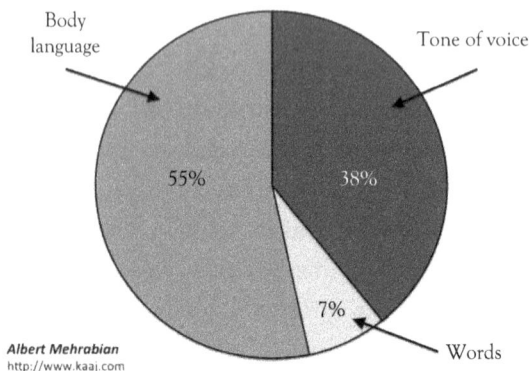

Albert Mehrabian
http://www.kaaj.com

This figure relates to studies carried out decades ago by Albert Mehrabian, Professor Emeritus of Psychology at UCLA (University of

California-Los Angeles). Professor Mehrabian's experiments dealing with communication of feelings and attitudes revealed that when there is a mismatch of what is being said with the way in which it is being said, we are more influenced by the tone and body language. I think it can be confusing when people explain this concept incorrectly. It is not the case that in every communication, only 7 percent of the meaning is attached to the words we say—it is only relevant in the context of the aforementioned study.

For more information about the studies, see Professor Mehrabian's website: www.kaaj.com/psych/

The simple thing to focus on here is that we communicate with our words, voice, and body—all of which need to be saying the same thing; otherwise, our audience does not believe us or are not persuaded.

For example, if you ask someone if they are okay and they reply: "I am fine" yet their body language and facial expression say otherwise, you are more likely to rely on the latter.

Similarly, if you say "I am so excited to be here" at the beginning of your presentation, but your face doesn't say the same thing, your audience can tell that you lack sincerity.

Just remember, when there is any inconsistency with what is being said and the way in which is being said, we are more likely to believe the underlying messages communicated through tone of voice, facial expressions, and mannerisms.

Confidence

Fear of speaking in public is quite common. You may not have any fear at all—some people don't. However, if this is an issue for you, then you are in good company. It is an irrational fear shared by many people and we don't always know why we feel this way.

If you are a fan of Jerry Seinfeld, here is an extract from the opening scene from a Jerry Seinfeld episode—season 4, episode 22 "the pilot" opening scene:

THE PILOT (1)

[setting: night club]

JERRY: To me, the whole concept of fear of success is proof that we are definitely scraping the bottom of the fear barrel. Are we gonna have to have AA-type meetings for these people? They'll go: "Hi, my name is Bill, and the one thing I'm worried about is to have a stereo and a cream-colored couch." According to most studies, people's number-one fear is public speaking. Number two is death. *Death* is number two! Now, this means to the average person, if you have to go to a funeral, you're better off in the casket than doing the eulogy.

(Transcribed by "The Maestro" Originally posted on The News Guys (Mike's) site http://www.geocities.com/tnguym—Permission is given to copy scripts to other sites, provided credits as two lines mentioned previously are included.)

According to Jerry, the number one fear we have is speaking!

I had a debilitating fear of public speaking for more than 30 years of my life. All through school, university, law school, and then, for almost half of my career, as a lawyer. It was so bad, just the thought of having to speak would make me physically sick, so that I wanted to throw up. I avoided every opportunity to present until one day I had no choice. I was asked to give a 10-minute update in a team meeting, and I literally froze. I felt so humiliated and angry with myself that I decided to do something about it. Over the next few years, I found some amazing speakers to learn from, and I joined a Toastmasters club to practice speaking in front of groups. It took me three months to gather up the courage to give my first speech at my club, but it was a positive step in a long journey to finding a way to get comfortable with speaking. I didn't know then what I know now.

It is possible to cope with these feelings and thoughts. By preparing well, we can take away some of the issues that can cause anxiety. Preparation is one of the best ways to tackle nerves about speaking in public. Most of us are not very good when we first start presenting. By finding more opportunities to speak, you build upon your experience and with that, comes increased confidence. You begin to realize it wasn't as bad as you thought.

The three things that helped me with my confidence in speaking were:

- Choosing to control my mindset
- Practicing continuously
- Putting the audience's interest first and focusing on their experience

You get what you focus on. What you think about determines how you feel. The way you feel can affect your physiology, and the opposite is also true. If you haven't come across Amy Cuddy's TED talk, "Your Body Language Shapes Who You Are," take a look—there are some fascinating tips on positive body postures to help with confidence:

www.ted.com/talks/amy_cuddy_your_body_language_shapes_who_you_are

Mindset

When we feel fearful about speaking in front of others, we go into a "fight or flight" state physiologically. Our bodies are hardwired to do this when we feel threatened. It was once helpful when needing to run away from a scary beast, but not so helpful in everyday life now. It is an unconscious response that happens on autopilot. But, here is the interesting thing about the physical and mental state we get into. That adrenalin rush is what makes us really alert. Heightened senses can help us achieve peak performance.

The physical symptoms of fear are the same as an adrenalin rush when we are excited about something. Learning to change the way you think about fear and reframing it to mean you are ready to do your best can help. What you believe about your ability to present has an impact on your outcome. What you say to yourself does the same—you get what you focus on.

Compare these two sentences:

"I want to deliver confidently, but I don't think I'm good enough…"

"I used to feel this way, but now I'm working toward feeling confident."

Just a simple shift in how you speak to yourself. When you talk in absolutes, you close off your mind. The other way opens up to possibilities.

It is completely understandable to not want to embarrass ourselves in front of peers. Fear of failing or embarrassment holds people back. We've all had embarrassing moments in our lives that we probably want to forget about. Sometimes, we can look back and laugh about them. My team meeting disaster was the thing that spurred me into action.

Developing confidence as a speaker is a process.

Visualization is also a powerful technique to help with confidence—check out the section on mental rehearsal in Chapter 8. In Chapter 11, we will also examine in more detail how to get in a resourceful state, so that you are ready to present on the given day.

Speaker Notes and Reading

When we think of presenters, the image that usually comes to mind is someone standing behind a lectern or podium reading out content from notes or slides. That may be the style for certain situations such as lecturers or teachers, but it isn't a style that engages a business audience. If someone can take your slides or notes away and read them, there is no point in you being there to present.

Nothing drains the life out of a presentation more than a speaker looking down with her or his head buried in their notes or script, reading. It can be a comfort to know that your script is written out in full and is there on the podium to refer to, should you lose your way in the presentation. However, under pressure, could you really find your spot in a sea of text? Probably not. This could really throw you off base.

Gradually move away from a full script to one sentence prompts or keywords on a card, so that they are easily available to jog your memory. Condense your notes to keywords written in large font on cue cards then staple them together so that they remain in the correct order even if you dropped them. Or, you could use your mind map that you created earlier and cleaned up. That can sit discreetly on the keyboard of the laptop you are presenting from and no one will see it.

PowerPoint and Keynote have a presenter mode that opens up a section in the bottom half of your screen to add notes only you can see as you are playing your slideshow. The good thing about this is that if you have the laptop screen positioned in front of you on a podium or table, you can remain facing the audience and just glance down when you need to check your notes. The ideal situation is still one where you are so familiar with your slide order and content that you do not need speaker notes.

Timing

Very few people have any idea of how much material they can cover in the time they are given to present—whether that is 10 minutes, 20 minutes, or longer. Quite often, they overestimate and produce too much content. When you structure your presentation, you can divide it into time segments.

Let's go back to Darren Tay's Toastmasters winning speech. The guidelines for this contest are very strict. The maximum amount of time any contestant can speak for is 7 minutes and 30 seconds. Even one second beyond this leads to the contestant being disqualified. Clearly, it was crucial for Darren to prepare in such a way as to ensure that he remained within the allotted time. After months of preparation, both in terms of writing the content and practicing the delivery, he knew down to within a few seconds where the key stages of the speech were. If you watch the speech, you see that about five minutes on the video timeline, he actually draws our attention back to his underpants worn over his suit to ask us in the audience whether five minutes is too long to be wearing the pants.

Here is the video link again: Darren Tay full video within Business Insider article:

http://uk.businessinsider.com/toastmasters-public-speaking-champion-darren-tay-2016-8/?r=US&IR=T/#-1

That level of preparation is arguably too excessive for you in your business preparation perhaps. But, it is important to prepare your material with accurate timings. Here are some guidelines:

- Know how long your material actually does take when spoken out loud at a normal conversational pace.
- Be aware that you will lose your audience if you go over time.
- Be able to adjust your content if other speakers go over or under time.
- Avoid running out of time and skipping slides at the end, as you will appear underprepared.
- Know where you want to end and how you can segue-way into it. Don't leave the audience hanging and disappoint them.

You may have spent time incorporating humorous stories into your planned presentation. When you deliver them in front of a live audience, you need to build in time to allow for laughs so that you don't step over them. Adrenalin has a big effect on timing. It causes us to speed up if we feel nervous. Make allowances for these scenarios. Plan to finish early so that you have some cushion. Your audience and event organizers will be thankful you did not go over time. Going over time has an impact—on catering, people needing to be elsewhere, and so on.

When you get into the habit of preparing your content to fit time slots, become familiar with your mini stories or vignettes, and gain a sense of how long you speak, you can be ready to speak off the cuff if asked. This might scare the pants off you right now, but when people see how good you are, they will ask you to speak more often.

Pace

There is a tendency to talk too fast when presenting—especially when nerves kick in as a result of the adrenaline rush. You might also do this unconsciously because you want to get it over with! Remember, this is all about the audience experience. Getting the pace or speed of your delivery right is important for them. No doubt you have seen this in action when other people have been speaking and you are literally willing them to slow down. There is something unsettling about this.

We think faster than we speak. You will be very familiar with what you want to say, but your audience is hearing your material in this way for the first time. Not only that, remember, you are not talking *at* the audience, you are having a conversation. They may not respond verbally, but they can acknowledge what you have shared with nonverbal cues such as nodding agreement, facial expressions, or simply thinking about what you have just said silently. The right pace allows this to happen.

Practice slowing down. You probably need to speak more slowly than you think you do.

Pause

The "power of a pause" is often described as a great technique for speakers. It will help slow you down and let the audience take in your comments. Give it room to breathe.

A pause of a couple of seconds might seem like an eternity to you, but for those in the audience it isn't. If you are not used to working with pauses, then practice so that they no longer feel artificial and awkward, but are necessary rest stops in your delivery.

Filler Words

In everyday conversation, we use filler words such as um, you know, like…, but we may not realize we are doing this throughout our presentations. A common habit is to use these words while we are thinking of what to say next. What is wrong with them? Nothing on the face of it, but it could be distracting for people in the audience. Becoming aware of what your particular fillers are is the first step. You can then take action to minimize them, forming a new habit such as using pauses instead.

Pitch and Volume

Add emphasis and drama through your voice. There is no point putting in all that work into crafting a great presentation if you deliver it in a boring flat tone of voice that never changes the whole time you are speaking. It would drain the energy out of the room. Change it up from time to time.

Newscasters are a good example. They have to remain neutral and simply report the news. However, it's not as easy as that. How they speak is not a monologue. They change the tone of their voice to match the context of the story or news piece. If you watch and listen closely, you'll notice that the tone for a serious piece is low and different from that used for a more light-hearted good news story where the voice becomes lighter and a little faster paced. You can literally hear the mood come through.

This is such a powerful way to keep your audience engaged. Remember, sameness and monotony are going to lead to losing audience attention.

Volume is another key factor. If you have a naturally quiet voice, then it is going to be a challenge to make yourself heard in the back row of the audience. If it's possible to use a microphone, then that works great because you can speak at your natural volume and still be heard. There is nothing worse than people not being able to hear a speaker—they get frustrated and lose interest.

It is not always be possible to use a microphone, so what then? I have a naturally quiet voice and have had to learn to project and speak by breathing from the diaphragm and not the chest. This was one of the things that going to Toastmasters really helped me work on—regular practice with breathing from the abdomen to help carry my voice.

Conversational

The best presenters and speakers are those who come across as conversational—emulating the way we talk to each other everyday. That will make you easy to listen to. It comes with practice. You don't want to talk at the audience or lecture them. We don't speak the way we write. Rather than trying to sound polished and professional, leave out words you would not use in everyday conversation—it will help you sound more natural.

The Power of "You"

"You" is a powerful word. Remember your presentation is about adding value for your audience, and so, they should be the focus. It can be really easy to deliver from an "I" focus. Bring the audience in more by changing up your phrasing to include them and using the word "you." This will ensure you don't talk at them. This is a dialog, not a lecture.

Body Language—Natural Style

Picking up on the conversational point, you want your delivery to be as natural as possible. That includes your body language and energy. It should also be congruent with your words.

Depending on what you read, some speaker coaches or experts will give you guidelines on body language such as standing in a certain way and using your hands in a certain way. I strongly believe that, to be authentic, what feels normal to you in terms of how you move is fine. The only caveat is that it must not be distracting for the audience.

Some speakers have very distracting styles, and quite often, they are not even aware that they are being distracting. There are those people who pace up and down the front of the room, and the audience feels like they are at a tennis match, having to turn their heads continuously to keep up with them.

Let me give you some other examples of distractions:

- Hands in pockets…jangling coins
- Playing with a pen—clicking it on and off
- Playing with hair or wedding rings

It can feel awkward not knowing what to do with your hands, and so holding a pen or playing with a ring helps keep the hands busy. Next time you present, focus on what you are doing with your hands and think about whether it is a distraction for the audience.

Standing still versus moving around? If you watch Ken Robinson's TED video, you'll notice he stands still, has a commanding presence, but connects with every part of the audience. Moving around and pacing the stage can work for some people—Steve Jobs did it in some of his presentations. What matters is whether it works for you and your audience.

Ken Robinson: Do Schools Kill Creativity:
www.ted.com/talks/ken_robinson_says_schools_kill_creativity

If there is a podium, get out from behind it—people trust you more when they can see you, remove the barrier. TED talks don't have podiums—speakers just stand in the middle of the stage.

Gestures are great to enhance a point as long as they aren't jerky or too frequent. In Chapter 3, we looked at Darren Tay, the 2016 champion of public speaking, as well as Ken Robinson. They have very different styles and use body language very differently, yet effectively.

If you watch Darren, he has very exaggerated facial expressions and uses his hands a lot. The audience is quite big with several hundred people, and so to connect with every part of the audience, he makes full use of the big stage—walking across it and addressing every part of the auditorium.

Going back to the previous newscaster example, not only do they change the tone of their voice, but there are subtle changes in the face to reflect the news piece. If you turned the sound off and watched the moving images, you could still tell if it was a serious or light-hearted news piece from the newscaster's expressions. A smile can go a long way to building a connection with the audience.

Making eye contact is important—this is a key part of connecting with and building rapport with people in your audience. Some speakers find this easy to do and others feel awkward. Think how awkward it feels when you are having a conversation with someone who avoids eye contact. It is weird, right? There could be any number of reasons why he or she is not able to look at you—they could be shy or evasive. Either way, it doesn't help the interaction. Connect with each corner of the room, making eye contact with someone in that region before moving on as you turn your attention to other parts of the audience. Once you've made eye contact with people, they are likely to listen more attentively.

Energy, Vitality, and Enthusiasm

If *you don't* seem interested in what you are sharing, why should they?! You set the tone in the room.

What does energy look like? Voice, gestures, smile… of course, not everyone can be like Tigger and that is not what is necessarily required. Obviously, if you walk into a room bouncing around being loud and there is silence in the room with serious somber expressions on the audience members faces, then there is going to be a mismatch. You have to be respectful of where they are and start by meeting them there before connecting with them and leading them through your presentation with your energy and enthusiasm.

With all of this, the best way to know how you come across is to get regular feedback.

Key Points

- Find you own authentic style.
- Your words, tone, and body language need to be congruent.
- Practice and shift your mindset to build confidence.
- Be conversational.
- Think about how your body language will be perceived by the audience and adjust your style, if appropriate.

Links

Professor Mehrabian's website:
www.kaaj.com/psych/
Amy Cuddy: Your Body Language Shapes Who You Are:
www.ted.com/talks/amy_cuddy_your_body_language_shapes_who_you_are
Darren Tay full video within Business Insider article:
http://uk.businessinsider.com/toastmasters-public-speaking-champion-darren-tay-2016-8/?r=US&IR=T/#-1
Ken Robinson: Do Schools Kill Creativity:
www.ted.com/talks/ken_robinson_says_schools_kill_creativity

CHAPTER 7

Humor

One of the main focuses of this book is to find ways to engage your audience. So far, we have covered the importance of stories and putting information into context so that it is easily understood.

Another way is to bring humor into your talk. You don't need to try and get a big laugh; you just want to allow the audience a way to connect with your material.

Have you ever considered opening with a joke? Only some people can pull this off, so it is probably only a good idea if you are good at telling jokes and it relates to your content. If you are telling one for the sake of it, then don't. Why would you risk it when you only have a few moments to make an impact—a good one? Comedians spend hours and days crafting a joke to make it their own. Then, they spend days and even months testing it in front of live audiences to see where the laughs are. You probably don't have that kind of time.

However, you can open with a humorous story. Great comedians build their jokes into a story.

Are there any topics where it isn't appropriate to add humor? Every video example I have used in this book so far to illustrate techniques has a serious message. The content has been serious—from suffering a stroke to being bullied. Yet, every single speaker in those videos has incorporated humor—they have taken us through a range of emotions to create contrast. You can make any topic funnier to lighten the mood.

You don't have to be naturally funny or crack a joke to add humor to your presentation. Just look at Ken Robinson. Watch how he uses his conversational style and everyday stories to make us laugh.

Let's look at the 2016 Toastmasters winning speech again. Darren Tay walks out onto stage, pauses, makes eye contact, and then pulls a pair of white underpants out from his pocket and puts them on—*over* his suit. He pings the elastic band for effect and then continues to stand there with his hands on his hips.

Without even saying anything, he gets a laugh from the audience. Why, because it is a funny sight and we didn't expect it. He begins the speech, and then a few moments into it, he teases the audience by reprimanding us for staring at the pants instead of looking at his eyes.

The safest type of humor is your story—having fun at your expense is less likely to offend anyone and makes you much more approachable. Embarrassing for you—funny for them. Even simple things such as having an accent—make a joke about that.

You could reference back to something funny said earlier by another speaker or refer to something in the news lately that is amusing.

Your Story File

Just like researching your material generally and capturing ideas for content and stories, collecting ideas for humor is no different. If you see or hear something funny, record it somewhere, so that you can use it later. Start building a list of funny incidents you have experienced or notice everyday—whether that is in conversations or watching a movie—anything. This is just about collecting thoughts at this stage. Pull stories from your life—past and present. Remember if you don't capture them, then they disappear into the brain attic somewhere!

You can always spin your humor to make it fit into your theme. On the face of it, how is talking about your four-year-old son's school play relevant to schools killing creativity? It is, when the lesson that you draw out from it is that: kids are not afraid to make a mistake, and yet, as they grow up, they lose that ability to try things for fear of failure.

The Element of Surprise

Taking a surprise turn or deliberately misdirecting your audience usually gets a laugh.

On January 9, 2007, Steve Jobs gave a keynote at the launch of the first iPhone. During his presentation, he demonstrated how to access

Google Maps on the phone, zoom in, and find the local Starbucks coffee shop. When the telephone number appeared on the screen, he clicked on it, and the phone dialed the shop. It was the first ever iPhone public call. When the unsuspecting barista answered and asked "Good morning, how can I help you?"

Steve said:

"Yes, I'd like to order 4000 lattes to go please,…just kidding. Wrong number. Goodbye." The entire auditorium burst out laughing. He had done something totally unexpected—made a prank call, live from the Moscone Center in San Francisco. Of course it wasn't just a whim—he had planned for it, but we in the audience would never know that. To this day, Apple fans remember that gag and try to recreate it whenever they are in the same coffee shop.

Steve Jobs calling Starbucks; the relevant part is at about 46 minutes into this video: www.youtube.com/watch?v=mqylGY_YSXA

When you write out your funny story, do so in full in the same way we discussed in the story chapter. Your editing process is the same—you keep cutting until you have only enough words and emphasis to get you to your punchline or point. Just as a comedian would craft a joke, get to the punchline as fast as possible.

Analogies and Examples

We looked at analogies in the story chapter, and even these can be funny. Here is an example:

Most people use PowerPoint as if they were driving a Ferrari at 20mph. It can do so much, but in the wrong hands, they may as well drive a station wagon.

Pictures and Video

You can also bring in the funny through pictures or video clips. Just remember to check copyright and be respectful of the company policies, and so on. Use Canva.com to create your own graphics, or take your own photos. A comparison between what's good and less good works quite well.

Key Points

- Start observing things that go on around you, in the media, and so on.
- Capture ideas and store them for later.
- Keep editing your humorous story until you get to the punchline as quickly as you can.
- Add an element of surprise or misdirection to get you to the punchline.
- Use pictures and video to add humor.

Links

Steve Jobs calling Starbucks—the relevant part is at about 46 minutes into this video:

www.youtube.com/watch?v=mqylGY_YSXA

Sir Ken Robinson

www.ted.com/talks/ken_robinson_says_schools_kill_creativity

Darren Tay, World Champion—Toastmasters Speech Contest 2016

http://uk.businessinsider.com/toastmasters-public-speaking-champion-darren-tay-2016-8/?r=US&IR=T/#-1

CHAPTER 8

Rehearsal and Feedback

Practice. Practice. Practice.

You need to put in the time to be confident of a decent result. It might sound old fashioned and boring, but there really is no substitute if you want to be great. This is what will get you to mastery. Great speakers are made, not born.

You could of course just wing it and be okay. If you are really committed to mastering presentation skills, you have to be able to take a look at yourself and the gap between where you are now and where you would like to be. When you watch someone who is great at speaking, know that they still work on getting better every single day. It never stops.

Some key benefits to spending time rehearsing:

- Overcoming fears of speaking
- Keeping to your time slot
- Becoming familiar with your slide deck and content
- Providing a better audience experience and giving value

I have referred to Steve Jobs a few times in this book. If you watch some of the Apple product launches going back over 20 years, you'll notice that even Steve gets visibly better over the years. He would have put in hundreds of hours of preparation for those product launch presentations over that time.

You don't have that many hours. Here's the thing, even if you put in just two hours of practice with two to three full run-throughs of your talk, you will be miles ahead of most other business presenters who will wing it. Typically, a lot of people focus too much on creating the slide deck and then think they can just use the slides as a teleprompter to keep them on track. They might spend a lot of money on designers, never thinking about proper preparation. There is almost an obsession about getting the slides right.

The more you practice, the more muscle memory you develop—like going to the gym and improving strength over many sessions. In your mind, you are creating stronger neural pathways, like the grooves in a vinyl record. When you build a strong foundation, you can relax in the knowledge that you know your content pretty well and have tested out how you deliver it, so that if something unplanned occurs, you can still cope with it.

This part of your preparation is extremely important. I can't stress that enough. I do know, however, that there may be resistance to this for two reasons:

- When too rehearsed, you come across as stilted. Think about actors. They spend weeks learning their lines; and then when they perform it's like it is for the first time, making it look effortless. It is the preparation that lets them be present, and in the moment, giving their audience a great experience. For that audience on that day, it will be the first time they see that performance.
- There just isn't enough time to devote to rehearsal. Remember presentations are an investment of time for both parties—the speaker and the audience. If they have given up valuable time to come and listen to you, don't they deserve something prepared to a high standard?

It is the practice that helps you sound spontaneous, so that in your presentation, you can check in with the audience and converse with them. Your rehearsal ensures you know your material really well and helps you iron out potential problems.

At the very least, learn to match your delivery with your slides. Otherwise, you risk losing your place. When that happens, it could have a dampening effect on your confidence, even if you are normally a confident speaker. If your slides let you down, you want to know you can still carry on.

At one of the law firms where I worked, we organized an annual conference for our clients at a prestigious location in London. The building itself was a big draw for our audience, as it had a lot of interesting history associated with it. The other big draw was a keynote speaker we had managed to persuade to speak at our event—he was one of the country's leading experts in his field. My job was to brief all the speakers and make sure they had everything they needed, including loading their slides onto the laptop in advance. Not only did this speaker send his slides to us at the last minute late the night before, he turned up five minutes before he was due to go on stage. There was no time for a briefing.

About 10 minutes into his presentation, he somehow managed to hit the keyboard on the podium and knock his slide presentation out of slide-show mode. He kept trying to use his clicker to move the slides on, but of course that can't happen if you are not in slideshow mode—he didn't know that because he clearly hadn't created his own slides and didn't know the basics of PowerPoint. It's an easy fix—just one click on the screen. But if you don't know that, then it can interrupt your flow, making you lose your place. Which is exactly what happened—there were a few awkward moments for him and the audience. I rushed onto the stage and fixed the slides quickly, but not before he became flustered.

These things happen to the best of us—you just need to find a way of keeping your cool and regular practice goes a long way toward that.

Rehearsal lets you ditch the script and learn how to connect with the audience. The whole of point of preparation is to become so familiar with your material that you can then relax and be fully present with your audience—avoiding common mistakes such as talking to the slides. Depending on how much time you invest in your preparation, you will know what is on the next slide or which point to talk about next without checking. You internalize your content, so that it becomes second nature.

Remember from the earlier section on designing slides—if you use mainly images and very little text, the audience will be looking at you and not reading from the slides. That means they expect you to acknowledge them and keep that connection going with your body language and eye contact.

Using Notes

There is nothing wrong with using notes in a presentation if that makes you feel more comfortable. Just be aware that every time you look at them, you lose eye contact with the audience and are in danger of break-ing the connection you have with them. People can sometimes interpret lack of eye contact as a sign of low confidence, dishonesty, or insincerity.

Rehearse with your notes, so that you know what it feels like to occasionally look down and yet still be able to keep eye contact and maintain a conversational tone.

Make the notes big, using only keywords and not a full script—that will help you avoid getting drawn into reading word for word. Have your notes out of sight on your laptop keyboard. That way they don't detract from your presentation. If you have speaker notes under your slides in the bottom half of the screen, try to keep your reliance on them to a mini-mum. To add notes to each slide, just scroll down under the actual slide and you will see a white box, which you can type straight into.

My own process for learning new content for a presentation looks like this:

- Brainstorming every possible angle on a blank sheet of paper.
- Storyboarding key ideas and stories, putting them in the right order.
- Scripting out new parts of my presentation—I already have preprepared stories so don't need to write them out or learn them.
- Rehearsing and recording my voice on my phone.
- Listening to my recording at every opportunity.
- Condensing my script into keywords in boxes on a single sheet of paper that can sit on a laptop keyboard.

That last step of getting my key points including the open and close onto one sheet of paper serves as my final roadmap. It's the framework I can use for a 10-minute talk or a 90-minute talk. I just add more examples and detailed explanations for the longer version, but my framework stays the same. I keep that sheet so I can use it again if I deliver that talk elsewhere.

This process helps me to become so familiar with my content I don't need the notes after a while. It may seem scary to lose the notes totally, but have a couple of run-throughs without them—you'll be surprised at how much you remember. Then you can use a note card with just a few key words as a prompt.

Memory Palace Part 2

Earlier, we looked at the concept of organizing your thoughts and the method of loci.

Put it into practice by using the technique to map out your talk. Use a physical location you are very familiar with, such as your home or a route you regularly travel to work or elsewhere. Hang your key points around your home in different rooms, like in the story of the Greek poet Simonides where he used the seating arrangement in the banquet hall to remember the diners. Or, use key markers along your chosen route, such as distinctive landmarks or buildings, and pin your key points in order at each location.

For example, your opening phrase could be written on the doormat or on the door before you enter your home. You can use symbols, photos, or paintings to hang your ideas on.

Once you have created this palace, walk through it in your mind. If you think you have very little time to prepare a presentation, this is a technique that can help you become more efficient. Putting something unfamiliar next to something we know very well helps us remember new information.

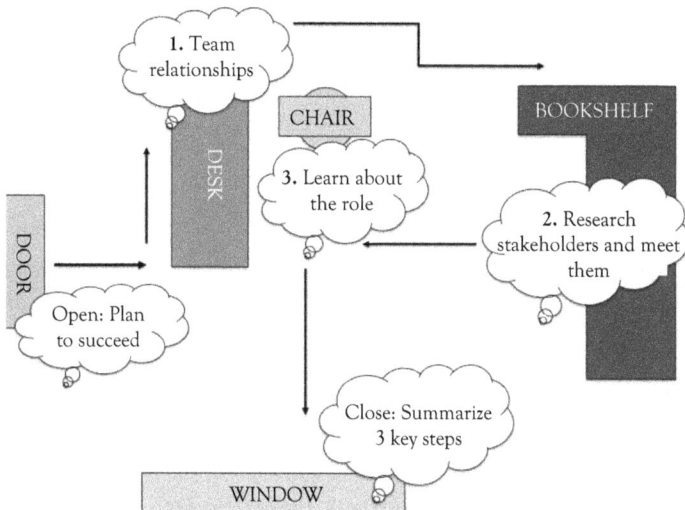

This is a simple example using the office layout to plot out key stages of a leadership talk to memorize the order of the speech. Replacing the text bubbles with distinctive or ridiculous images will make it even more memorable.

Blank Screen and Remote Clickers

A great way to bring the audience attention back to you once your current slide has served its purpose is to blank the screen. You can do this by pressing "B" on your keyboard—this will give you a black screen. To get back to your slides, just press the same key again and you can continue with the slide show. If you want a white screen instead, use the "W" key in the same way. Practice using this when you rehearse—mainly because you get used to remembering to switch your slides back on again on the actual day!

Using a remote clicker can free you up to move around the room without being tied to the podium. It will let you be more natural in your delivery, and getting out from behind a podium creates a better connection with the audience, as there is no barrier between you and them. Again, something to rehearse with.

Quality Feedback

Improving as a presenter is all about getting quality feedback and making necessary adjustments to keep honing your craft. For that to happen, you want to get good-quality feedback.

Something really important to remember is that feedback is someone else's perception of what they saw, heard, or felt. It is useful information for you to have, but what you then choose to do with it is up to you.

Being self-aware of how you come across and understanding how people feel around you is very powerful.

Let's talk about feedback in general. Every time you present to an audience, you get feedback whether you consciously notice it or not. At a very basic level, the feedback you get is the reaction in the room through facial expressions, body language, and questions from the audience. If you hand out feedback or comment sheets (sometimes called happy sheets), you may gain some additional insights.

The limitation of these kinds of feedback forms is that they are dependent on the individual audience member being honest and detailed enough. Plus, of course, the response you get is influenced by the set of questions included on the form. These sorts of forms are filled at the end of a seminar when people are getting ready to leave or move on to the refreshments part of the event.

There is generally a scoring section that looks similar to the following example:

Evaluation		
5	☑	Outstanding
4	☐	**Very Good**
3	☐	**Good**
2	☐	**Satisfactory**
1	☐	**Poor**

It might be nice to get a high score of excellent or similar, but what does that really tell you? Someone's version of excellent is not that same as the next person's. It is still valuable to collect this type of information because you can get a sense check of going in the right direction.

Read on for more valuable ways of getting quality feedback.

Video Recording

The best way to see and hear what others will is to video record yourself practicing your presentation. It will give you the opportunity to listen to your material as spoken out loud, as well as see what you are doing with your body language. You could just use you smartphone or laptop to do this. No one else needs to see it if you don't want to share it, and you can delete it afterward. You could also keep it stored somewhere to reflect back on and see how much you have progressed over time.

You may find that you need to exaggerate your movement and gestures—what we think is going on in our minds often is not really how it plays out. It's a similar concept to using pauses—what seems like an eternity to us is really only one or two seconds in reality.

Feedback from Colleagues

Get feedback from peers whose opinion you respect. Rehearse in front of them and get them to ask you questions, so that you can practice that part as well. This also works really well for a pitch presentation—your dress rehearsal with the team can be a useful opportunity to test tough questions that may come up from the audience.

Mental Rehearsal

Visualization, sometimes referred to as mental rehearsal or imagery, is a very powerful technique.

What it is: Basically, it's a technique for using your imagination to create the outcome you want. It's like a mental warm up.

In her book, *Creative Visualization,* Shakti Gawain gives lots of practical advice on how to use visualization. She first wrote the book in 1978 and has since sold several million copies worldwide. It falls into the self-help category, which perhaps not everyone is open to; however, you may want to check it out.

For those of you who are interested in more research-based evidence, we can look at the sports industry. Many top sporting stars have openly shared about their mental preparation in the lead up to major games or events. The use of imagery—rehearsing a positive mental experience to enhance their ability to achieve a desired outcome—has been the practice of sporting legends from boxer Muhammad Ali to tennis player Andy Murray.

Visualization is not just something that is only found in the self-help section of the bookstore. Golfer Jack Nicklaus said he never hit a shot before visualizing it first. According to *Harvard Medical Magazine* (Susan Karcz, editor), it is commonly used by sports psychologists and coaches today:

https://magazine.hms.harvard.edu/play/competitive-edge

Michael Phelps, USA Olympic champion with 23 Olympic gold medals, is arguably one of the most successful athletes ever. In his book, *No Limits* (Michael Phelps and Alan Abrahamson—Simon and Schuster 2008), he talks about his rigorous training routine which consists of eating, swimming, weight training, and sleeping. He also describes something else—visualization. He imagines the perfect race in minute detail—every stroke.

For Michael Phelps, visualizing is an essential part of his preparation—to visualize how he wants things to go and also imaging scenarios that could go wrong, so that he can be prepared. He can have a plan. Since that book came out, Michael retired in 2012 and then came back out of retirement for the 2016 Olympics building on an already amazing record and career.

If this technique works for world-class athletes, why can't it help you and me? Try the following visualization exercise.

Visualization Exercise

- First, close your eyes and relax.
- Set the scene and see your presentation in detail, so that you are absolutely clear about what you have to do.
- In a relaxed state, see yourself as if watching on a big movie screen, as you are about to give your presentation exactly as you want it to go. See yourself in this picture as you are about to speak to your audience.
- Make the scene as perfect as you want it, but imagine in detail where you are standing or sitting, what the room looks like, the lighting, the furniture. See what clothes you are wearing and who else is in the room with you. Use your senses to make the details as rich as possible—vivid colors and sounds. What do you see? What do you feel? What do you hear?

- Now, you can step into the scene and imagine delivering the presentation for real in the present tense as if it is actually happening now. This time you are actually within the picture—look at the scene through your own eyes. See what you would see, hear what you would hear. Notice how well the audience is reacting to you. Really ramp up the senses and add intensity to the pictures, sounds, and feelings.
- This is your mind movie that you can replay over and over again.

Some people find it difficult at first to use this technique—they struggle to close their eyes and bring up clear images. That's okay—you don't have to see images in your mind for this process to work. If you don't see pictures, you may get a feeling or sense of what the scenario might look like. Earlier in Chapter 2, we looked at the way people process information in their own preferred way—they may be visual (pictures), auditory (sound of the audience applauding loudly), or kinesthetic (a feeling of confidence or sense of achievement). The imagined scenarios can include any of the senses.

To put it more simply, we all use our imaginations all the time and so this is nothing new. What I'm suggesting here is that if used consciously with deliberate intent, it can help increase your confidence in speaking and help you improve your delivery.

Much of the time we operate on autopilot, unconsciously going about our day without taking a few moments to check in with ourselves as to what outcome we want. Whichever way you approach this technique is fine. The most important thing to remember is to use multiple senses— sights, smells, sounds. The more detailed your imagined scenario, the better.

Of course, just like sitting on the couch imagining doing abdominal exercises to get a six pack won't work without putting in some physical effort, you can't create a great presentation without preparation. The practical and the imagination processes together strengthen your performance. That is why, the rest of this chapter walks you through the benefits of physical rehearsal.

Tripping Up

Don't sweat the small stuff—all this preparation will help you cope with things going wrong. Your ability to recover is the key to maintaining audience connection and their confidence in you.

Should something go wrong on the presentation day, don't apologize. Just acknowledge it, if it is something technical for example, and move on. If you left out some of your content, most of the time no one notices as only you know what you forgot to say. You can always bring it in later and say something like "just going back to that last point…" or save it for the Q&A section and slot it in there.

Long Term

I have mentioned Toastmasters International (www.toastmasters.org) a few times—both from my own experience and through the 2016 world champion's winning speech. If you haven't come across Toastmasters before, it is a nonprofit international organization comprised of speaking clubs in every major city in the world. It is the best-value personal development program you can get these days. You can pretty much find a club that suits your location at a time that works for you. They run most evenings of the week and sometimes as breakfast or lunch meetings. Many companies start their own clubs in-house just for staff. Check out their web link for more information.

The great thing about these clubs is they provide an opportunity to work on your speaking skills in front of a live audience who are encouraging and will give you feedback. There is a misconception that this kind of speaking club attracts members who are already good at giving speeches. That's not true. People come from all walks of life and all types of professions—from executives to students. Most people who come along for the first time are nervous about speaking. There are a few who are confident, but want to learn how to write speeches or incorporate humor. You also learn how to think on your feet and speak off the cuff.

When you have a framework, you can learn to wing it within that structure.

If you want to work on your skills outside of work, then finding a Toastmasters club could really help to ramp up your skills. Other ways in which you can find opportunities to practice some more are by asking to take a slot at a team meeting or even just asking a question at a conference in a room with a large audience. There is absolutely no substitute for a live audience to practice in front of.

Call Backs

When you are so well prepared and can be fully present in the moment, there are even more things you can do to increase your impact. If you are in a lineup of other presenters, making reference to what someone else said earlier will help you connect better with the audience, especially if it was something funny. You can benefit from the earlier reaction from the audience by reminding them of that moment. This is referred to as a "call back." You can do something like this only if you are relaxed enough to sit through other presentations and listen without worrying about your upcoming presentation.

Timing

One really important benefit of rehearsing is being able to speak for the time you have been allocated—no more, no less. If you go over, your audience won't thank you. Without walking through your entire talk and speaking it out loud, how would you know how long the entire thing will last? With experience, prepared vignettes, and so on, you can get a fair idea, but most of us can't be that accurate on time without testing our material fully. If you are over or under on timings in rehearsal, you can go back and adjust your material.

Sometimes, you will be given even less time than you prepared for because the previous speaker went on too long or an additional item suddenly appeared on the meeting agenda. Your preparation will help you trim material and fit in the new time slot. You will know how long each segment is and can decide which ones to cut, so that your key take away still makes sense—you are still able to take your audience from A to B, as discussed in Chapter 2.

Finally, build in a one-to-two-minute cushion, so that you aim to finish slightly earlier than your total time slot. When you give your presentation live, it may take you longer to get through your material.

Key Points

- Rehearse to feel more confident and remember your material better.
- Record your rehearsal on video, so that you can see and hear what the audience will experience.
- Practice in front of colleagues and test out tough questions the audience might ask.
- Try the visualization technique to help with confidence.
- Use the memory palace technique to remember your key points.
- Know the timings of every segment of your talk, so that you know where to cut on short notice.

Links

Harvard Medical Magazine
https://hms.harvard.edu/news/harvard-medicine/harvard-medicine/play/
    competitive-edge
Toastmasters International
www.toastmasters.org

Books

Gawain, S. 2002. *Creative Visualization*. Uttarakhand, India: Natraj Publishing.
Phelps, M., and A. Abrahamson. 2008. *No Limits*. New York, NY: Simon and Schuster.

CHAPTER 9

Q&A

Handling or dealing with questions, whichever way you like to describe it, is the most worrisome part for many of us. It's one thing to put in hours and effort crafting something amazing and then deliver it in style but, quite another to field curve ball questions! Not being prepared for questions can derail your presentation.

Let's look at it another way. The Q&A part of a presentation is an opportunity for you, as the expert, to showcase the depth of your knowledge and give a deeper insight into your personality, so that your audience can see what it might be like to work with you. It is also an opportunity for the audience to get further clarification of their own interests or issues. The question part could actually elevate your presentation and add value.

Keep in mind, the audience participants are more interested in having their questions answered than they are in your content.

The good news is you can prepare for questions. Think of it as preparing for a trial in court. When I first qualified as a lawyer, I remember being absolutely terrified of going to court because I had such a debilitating fear of public speaking. Added to that, I was quite often the most junior lawyer in the room. Not only did I have to worry about questions from the judge that I may not be able to answer, but I had to deal with other lawyers representing their own clients who would want to trip me up. Those were some of the most stressful experiences of my career.

After a while, I developed a coping strategy—I prepared for curve ball questions by putting myself in the judge's shoes or that of my opponents. I would think like they did, to help me work out questions they might come up with and then prepare my material. That really helped with my confidence. After a while, you get into the habit of thinking like that—viewing the situation from the other parties' perspective and antic-ipating their concerns or points of interest.

Here are some ideas for you to develop your own strategy, whatever the situation.

When to Take Questions

Set yourself up for success. Decide how you want to handle any questions and then let your audience know—guide them. You may want to take questions after each main section, leave them to the end as most people do, or take them ad hoc throughout your talk.

Taking questions after each section can be really useful if the content is complicated. Pausing to ask if there are any questions so far gives the audience a chance to process what has just been shared and gives you a chance to reset or take stock. Quite often, people do have questions, but are reluctant to ask in open forum for fear of sounding stupid or asking an "obvious question." This is where your research and preparation can be leveraged to full effect. You can slip in some extra material by framing it with "I often get asked," or "most people tend to …." A brief interaction at these stages can help keep them engaged.

Taking questions after each section, however, could disrupt the flow of the presentation, but may be appropriate depending on the type of meeting. You would also need to keep the presentation on track skillfully and steer away from lengthy discussions that take you away from the main theme.

Taking questions at the end is what we generally see in business pre-sentations or at conferences. The advantage is that you can take the audi-ence through your presentation without interrupting the flow. However, you need to make sure you keep your audience engaged with your con-tent and delivery if you are not pausing for interim questions.

How can you be ready for dealing with questions? Anticipate them.

Anticipating

Remember all the research you carried out earlier when identifying the rel-evant audience before structuring the content to make it as custom-made as possible? There will undoubtedly be material you eventually decided not to use in the final content. Hold it in reserve.

That same research data will help you identify the key issues that are important for your audience. Ideally, you will have built the content around the main areas of concern for them—answering questions up front.

This is the raw material mind map from the brainstorming stage in Chapter 2 (See example below)—all that research can be used for dealing with questions or covering material you left out of the main presentation.

When you have a good understanding of the audience's interests and level of existing knowledge, you will have a better idea of the type of questions they might ask.

Think through all possible questions that could come up, from basic to tricky and even hostile. Plan your answers and then rehearse them in the same way you would your presentation.

Trouble-Makers in the Audience

Just to be clear, I wouldn't suggest we make an assumption that there will be someone in the room who is on a mission to derail your presentation. However, there may be individuals in your audience who like to be controversial or have a pet subject or preoccupation. Some people may want to challenge you publicly. Handle these situations firmly and with humor if you can. Keep your composure—rely on your preparation to keep you grounded.

Be Concise

Getting drawn into long answers takes you off point and poses the danger of losing those members in the audience who are not interested in that point. Keep your answers short and to the point. If the audience wants more detail, they will ask a follow-up question.

You can weave in extra content if you invite questions, but there is little response. Just be careful to keep the balance—rather than using it as an opportunity to squeeze in more material, just share enough to answer a hypothetical question.

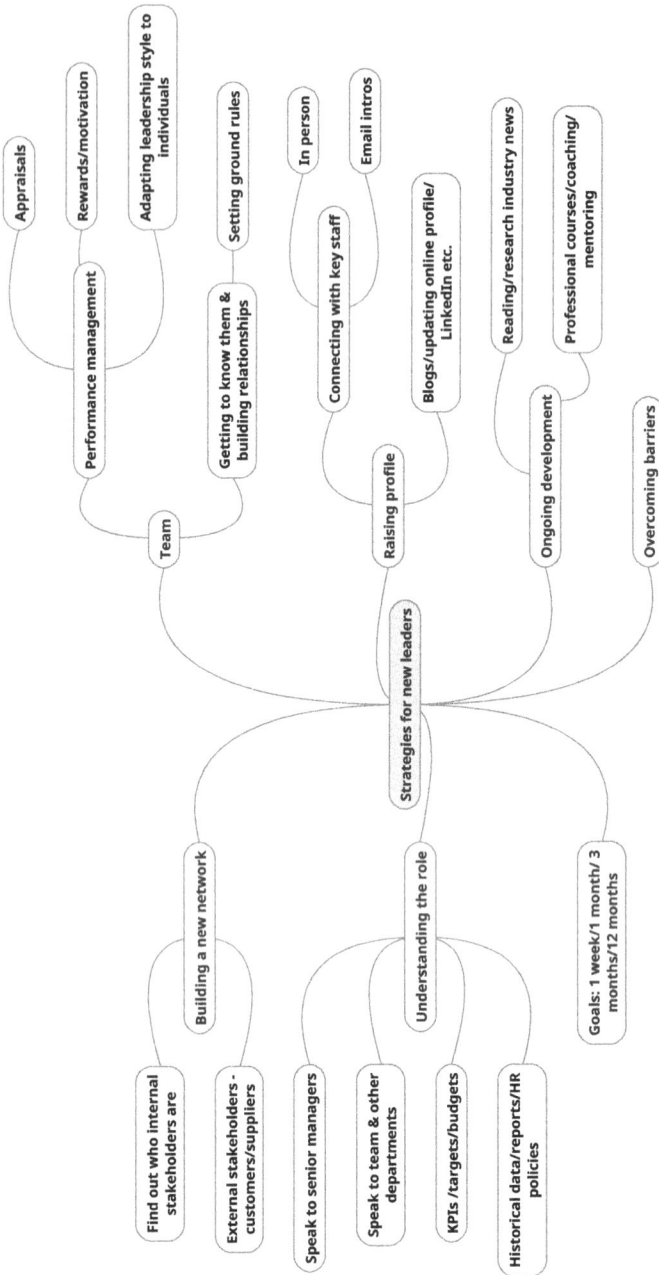

Strategies for new leaders

- Team
  - Performance management
    - Appraisals
    - Rewards/motivation
    - Adapting leadership style to individuals
  - Getting to know them & building relationships
    - Setting ground rules
- Raising profile
  - Connecting with key staff
    - In person
    - Email intros
  - Blogs/updating online profile/ LinkedIn etc.
- Ongoing development
  - Reading/research industry news
  - Professional courses/coaching/ mentoring
- Overcoming barriers
- Building a new network
  - Find out who internal stakeholders are
  - External stakeholders - customers/suppliers
  - Speak to senior managers
- Understanding the role
  - Speak to team & other departments
  - KPIs /targets/budgets
  - Historical data/reports/HR policies
- Goals: 1 week/1 month/ 3 months/12 months

How to Respond

Okay, so you have prepared as much as possible with reserve material and have decided at what stage of your presentation you will invite questions. But, how to respond? The following tips may help with any anxiety you might have about responding to potential unknown questions:

- Pause for a moment and take your time. This demonstrates that you are giving a considered answer, rather than jumping straight in.
- Listen carefully and repeat the question to buy yourself some time to think.
- Unpack questions with layers. People often raise several points wrapped up in one sentence. Listen for this and separate out the points by repeating them back. You might even want to take notes, so that you can select specific parts to answer and don't risk overlooking anything.
- Clarify the question. Some people tend to ramble on when they ask questions, or they have a particular interest and like to make statements or share opinions, rather than ask a question. In that case, pin them down and ask what their question is. Repeating or paraphrasing the question ensures you are both on the same page and not at cross purposes. In a large room, repeating the question may be necessary, as others may not have heard.
- Consider the perspective of the person asking the question. What would prompt them to ask it? Put yourself in their shoes. Does something need further clarification or more detail? Or, do they want to be more visible by asking a question in open forum? Asking questions or raising discussion points in this way can help raise profile and recognition of thought leadership among peers and colleagues.

When You Do Not Know

After all your preparation, there may still be questions that you just cannot answer in that moment. Most of us realize that no one has all the answers in a particular moment. It is okay to say you don't know. We probably know where to find the answer and can deal with it later.

Decide how you will deal with the "I don't know" scenario in advance. Do not wing it—the audience will see through that.

Rehearse your version of "I don't know." That could be "I'll check that out and get back to you," or "it's been a while since I looked at that; can I follow up with you later?" or something along those lines. The main thing is to say you don't have the answer immediately with confidence and certainty.

There will be times when questions touch on your weak areas, for example, when pitching a new product or service that has not yet been tested fully. Prepare for this and rehearse some phrases that indicate you acknowledge it is a weak area and are working on it, rather than becoming defensive or trying to tenuously justify your position.

If you feel confident enough, you can throw it out to the audience and ask if anyone else has come across that particular issue. Great tactic if you have team members in the room that can field specialist questions. Make sure you brief everyone beforehand on potential questions and warn them they may be called upon! Another way to look at this tactic is that someone else offering an opinion could get a discussion going. This extended discussion can be quite beneficial, and if it is after your main presentation has ended, it won't interrupt the flow.

Whichever way you handle questions, be respectful of your audience. Be aware of your tone of voice, body language, and delivery in the same way we have talked about for the main presentation. Even if a question seems ridiculous or has been covered already, acknowledge it in a professional way with a neutral tone of voice. The same goes for controversial or provocative comments.

Your mindset is the key. Be positive. Resist assuming that they are trying to trip you up.

Closing Stages

Finish strong. End your presentation with your call to action or conclusion. This keeps the energy high.

That means allowing for questions before your final conclusion or close. You want to leave a powerful final impression, and leaving your question section to the very end does not set you up for success. Save your summary slide as a lasting impression.

Key Points

- Think of questions as an opportunity for you to showcase your expertise.
- Remember, it is an opportunity for the audience to get their questions answered—put yourself in their shoes to anticipate what kind of questions could come up.
- Use your mind map from the brainstorming phase to help you prepare for questions.
- Rehearse taking questions and decide when or if you will take them, so you can let the audience know up front.
- Practice your version of "I don't know," so that you can feel confident and not worry about getting caught out.

CHAPTER 10

Handouts and Giveaways for the Audience

This chapter covers what to do about any information you may want to give to your audience either during the presentation for reference or to take away with them later.

Printed Slides

Quite often, attendees at business seminars will be given printed slides as handouts. The thinking behind this is that the audience can follow along with the slide presentation and make any notes they wish to add alongside the relevant slide. There is also an assumption that they will have something tangible and valuable to take away that will act as a quick reference guide at a later date.

That assumption is flawed. Slides do not make good handouts. Truncated text makes no sense without you, the speaker there, to put it all into context. We have already looked at the creation of slides for the benefit of the audience and the fact that they are your support act. If you do your job right, then the slides will not work without you!

As mentioned in previous chapters, a common mistake many presenters make is including lots of text in their slides, so that when they are printed, the attendees have some meaningful information. The problem is that not only is too much text on the actual slide distracting for the live audience, when they are printed the text is too small as seen in the example below. This is particularly bad, as handouts are often printed three slides to one sheet. What looks clear on the big screen does not translate well into the smaller hard copy version.

I hope, by now, I have convinced you not to use the slides as an information dump or as handouts for all of these reasons.

So, what can you do instead?

Parcel delivery

Key steps

_____
_____
_____
_____
_____
_____
_____

Parcel delivery protocol

- Anyone answer the door? Yes = hand over and get signature. No = possibly leave with neighbor
- Leave with neighbor? Yes = hand over parcel and get signature. No = possibly leave in safe place
- Leave in safe place? Yes = post blue slip through door. No = post white collection slip through door

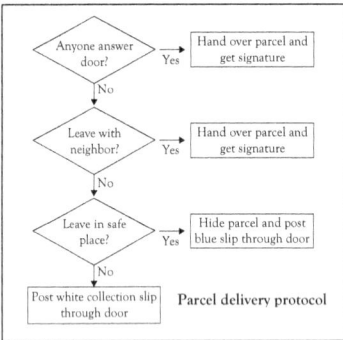

_____
_____
_____
_____
_____
_____

Anyone answer door? → Yes → Hand over parcel and get signature
↓ No
Leave with neighbor? → Yes → Hand over parcel and get signature
↓ No
Leave in safe place? → Yes → Hide parcel and post blue slip through door
↓ No
Post white collection slip through door   **Parcel delivery protocol**

_____
_____
_____
_____
_____
_____

Reports and Articles

Instead of printing text-heavy slides, repurpose that content and type it into an article or report, which the delegates can read later. It will serve as a standalone reference guide and also keep you front of mind—every time they look at that report, they will remember you. You will have all the material you need anyway from the preparation stage. All you are doing is putting your text into a text document and tidying it up with headings and maybe some branding.

This brief report is a much more valuable take away for your audience. You can leave them on the chairs before the presentation begins or hand them out at the end. The benefit of waiting until the end is that you are more likely to have their undivided attention—giving out papers usually results in people flicking through them! Make sure you tell them that a detailed handout will be distributed at the end and they do not, therefore, need to take notes. For those who do feel the need to make notes, have some blank paper available.

If it is a high-profile event and there is the budget to do so, you might want to create branded booklets or put your material into folders. Another idea is to create a laminated fact sheet or similar with just the key points as a quick reference guide that can sit on someone's desk.

Making a feature out of your take away will enhance the perceived value.

Paper Handouts Versus Digital Documents

These days, many organizations strive to be paperless—they only print what is necessary. With that in mind, you may want to rethink your approach to providing handouts. A great alternative is to e-mail your article or report after the presentation. That way you have another touch point with each individual member of the audience. This works really well if you are presenting to prospective clients. They get to see you in action during the presentation and get a feel for what it would be like to work with you. Then, when you follow-up with the report via e-mail, they hear from you again—keeps you of front of mind.

E-mailing content following the presentation works just as well for internal presentations in front of colleagues—e-mailing content gives people the option to store it in their own digital folders.

On a more practical note, think of all the trees you are saving by not printing handouts that either sit on a shelf never to be picked up again or get put in the trash or recycling when people get back to their desk. The other advantage of following-up in this way is that you can also include other material or messages such as forthcoming events or key dates. If your marketing department wants to collect feedback, you can link to an online survey within the same e-mail.

You might also want to record the event and send a link to the video file. This is a great option for following-up with people who couldn't make it to the event.

Different Types of Presentations

Formal presentations and seminars are not the only scenarios in which you may be speaking or presenting. You might be involved in team or board meetings or client pitches. In those situations, a printed document is helpful for your audience, particularly if you are talking numbers. Charts, spreadsheets, and so forth are difficult to see and process when put onto slides. You might want to take your audience through very detailed figures or workflows, giving everyone their own copy of visual content makes this easier.

Remember, just like your thinking behind creating beautiful slides, produce handouts that demonstrate clearly and effectively the point you want to get across. Resist the temptation to cram too much into one page or chart. The handouts are meant to support your point and make things easier for your audience to follow.

Key Points

- Printed slides don't mean anything without you, the presenter, explaining them, so ditch those types of handouts.
- Prepare a report or article instead of printing hard copies of your slides.
- E-mail the report after the event to create another touch point and remain in front of mind.
- Use printed hard copies of charts and spreadsheets where the data is too small to read on the screen.

CHAPTER 11

Logistics and Toolkit

You've prepared for your presentation as much as possible and now it's time to actually show up and deliver it. Arrive early so that you can check everything is right for you—even if it is in your own office building. However much you plan, things can still go wrong on the day of your presentation; anticipating them will help minimize any potential problems.

These are the aspects you will want to double check in order to be ready:

- Your content—slides, mind map, and backup slides
- Materials for the participants
- Environment—lighting, seating, screen
- AV (Audio Visual) support
- Equipment such as flip chart paper and pens
- Distractions
- Getting in the zone

Slides and Notes

Be prepared for tech failure. It is always safer to use your own laptop to avoid these issues.

However, this isn't always possible. Sometimes, you have to e-mail your slide deck over to someone in advance, and they will set it up ready for you to just come in and take your speaking slot at the designated time. If you are sending your presentation ahead of time to an event host or a colleague who is taking care of setting up your slides on the computer you will be using for the actual presentation, then there are a few things to be aware of.

If you are using video or audio clips, send those together with any images you inserted within the same digital folder as your slide deck as an attachment to your e-mail. It is always safer to have everything in one place in case something didn't save properly within your slides or gets moved out of place.

Most people use a version of PowerPoint to create their slide deck. Over the years, there have been many different versions of the software released. Slides don't always travel well. Different versions of PowerPoint can cause major problems on the presentation day. Incompatibility with the computer at the host venue if you are going offsite, or even going to the conference room in your own building can result in slides not sizing themselves correctly on the screen or images moving out of place. You can, of course, take care of the risk of images shifting out of place by grouping them and locking them in on each slide as discussed in Chapter 5.

Save your presentation with all your images, audio, and video clips onto a memory stick and take it with you. That way if your e-mailed version is not working quite right, you can use the saved version on your memory stick.

Let me give you some background on this. In the past, when I have hosted multispeaker events, speakers send me all kinds of slide formats via e-mail—some are more familiar with using PowerPoint design than others. Sometimes, what happens is that a few things are misaligned or don't show on a particular slide. Unless the misalignment is obvious I won't know anything is wrong and can't fix it when I load all the slides onto the presentation laptop in the conference room. When the speakers arrive, they can get upset if things aren't perfect; very often, there is no time to make last-minute changes, as the event is about to begin or the speaker didn't bring a backup.

Take a copy of your mind map or print out your slides, so that you can use them as a template if you have a complete tech failure.

If you are using notes or just want them in case of a brain freeze, make sure you prepare them in such a way that you can read them with a quick glance. Seems obvious to go over this again, but some key words written in big, bold font will help you much more than typed up sheets of paper.

Handouts or Materials for the Audience

We discussed in Chapter 10 about the merits of printing slides versus creating a report or article that has much more value. If you are going to hand out printed copies of the article or report, remember to let the audience know they will get something at the end of your talk and need not take notes if they don't want to. You could, of course, put them on the chairs at the beginning before everyone arrives, but then the handout could be a distraction—too much temptation to thumb through it.

If you e-mail any material to your host or organizer for printing, then check it when you arrive. I have been caught out a few times when pages have been missed or someone just forgot to print anything. Even if you cannot resolve the situation before you start your presentation, at least you can let the audience know what to expect.

If you have any promotional materials for your organization, such as branded pens or leaflets, that you want to hand out, then decide how you want to deal with that. Do you leave them at the back of the room or put them on chairs?

In Chapter 8, we discussed the benefit of handing out questionnaires for the audience to complete after your presentation to give you feedback. As I said before, the value in these types of feedback or comment sheets depends on how you design them. Sometimes, these things are out of your control—they have been designed by the learning and development team, and everyone has to use them or your host or event organizer has their own version. If you have any influence in these things, consider what questions you would ask that would give you useful data about whether your audience got any value from the presentation, as well as what they thought of your delivery style.

You could instead create an electronic survey, for example, using a platform such as SurveyMonkey (www.surveymonkey.com) and put a link to that into your follow-up e-mail when you send them your article or report. That might work better than trying to get people to fill in a comment sheet at the end when they might want to rush away following the presentation. The results of the online survey also can be electronically tabulated for easy reference.

Take a look at these sample questions:

	Strongly disagree	Disagree	Neutral	Agree	Strongly agree
The presenter knew what they were talking about	◯	◯	◯	◯	◯
The presenter connected with the audience well	◯	◯	◯	◯	◯
The presenter was able to explain things clearly	◯	◯	◯	◯	◯
It made me think of things in a new way	◯	◯	◯	◯	◯
I found the presentation useful	◯	◯	◯	◯	◯

Environment

If you can, check that the audience members are able to see the screen from every angle in the room. You might need to adjust the blinds or move some chairs.

You can't, of course, always do anything about these things if you are at someone else's offices or at a conference center, but it's good to arrive early and check it all out. That way you know whether the big screen is in the center of the stage and that if you walk in front of it you will block the audience's view, or worse, depending on where the projector is, have the images beamed onto your face if you stand in the wrong place.

I always like to see the room in advance if I haven't presented there before. I guess it's because I had that scare during my first international speaking opportunity! We sometimes take things for granted and then simple things, such as where the laptop will sit or the lack of a remote clicker, can throw us off.

Many hotels and conference venues have images or even 360-degree views of their meeting rooms. If I can, I take a look at that in advance. I also have asked my contact who has arranged for me to come and speak to take a photo of the meeting room and e-mail it to me. I think it is important to know what you are working with.

AV Support

I have learned the hard way that finding out who the AV guys are is vital—whether that is for internal or external presentations. I've organized enough multispeaker conferences as well as speaking at them to know that your tech support letting you down is one less thing you want to think about as you are getting in the zone ready to present. Meet with them early and go over some checks with them. When we turn up somewhere to speak, we assume someone else is taking care of all the other stuff. Please don't make that assumption—connect with whomever you need to and make sure you are all set up.

I'm referring to basic things such as which way the clicker advances slides—pick it up and check that you know how it works. I know, you're thinking this is pretty basic...they can only go one of two ways: left or right. In the middle of your presentation, with adrenaline rushing, will you know which way if you didn't check? I've seen too many speakers get caught by this simple thing—it interrupts their flow and they stand there looking helpless for a few moments. Remember my story about the expert who was completely lost when the slide show came out of presenter view?

If you are wearing a lapel microphone or carrying a handheld one, do you need to switch it on just before you get up to speak or will someone help you with this. You need to have access to the presentation room when the audience is not in there, so that you can go through a sound check with the AV guys. Even if you have rehearsed with a microphone, it is always beneficial to go through a sound check on the day and check for sound feedback, so that you know what adjustments to make before it is your turn to speak.

Go over to the laptop and click through your slides if the audience hasn't arrived in the room. Do they look okay, and if you play any media clips, are the speakers on?

If you want to show a video clip through an Internet connection or access websites and so on, then again, check that it all works. This is something else I found out the hard way. You generally get wireless access in external meeting rooms as part of the room contract, but the problem is that sometimes it's not a good connection. There may be another network you can connect to or you could use your own hotspot tethered to your phone for example. Personally, I avoid relying on Internet content, and wherever possible, use material that can be downloaded, copyright permitting.

Hopefully, these days, connectivity is not that bad. If you are using interactive apps, such as Glisser (https://glisser.com) or Sli.do (www.sli.do), you want everyone to be able to have a great network connection. Make sure you are not in a dark spot—the fantastic idea of audience interaction might not work. You could prepare for this by going low tech and running your polls or quizzes by asking for a show of hands or collecting votes on slips of paper then writing the results on a flip chart.

Never ever try something new on the day of your presentation. One of the reasons why I strongly recommend rehearsing is to avoid these mishaps.

Equipment

Many of your speaking opportunities will be in smaller meeting rooms in your office building or similar. You might not have someone to ask about AV, so it's good to have some backup for yourself in terms of any equipment you might use.

I think remote clickers are great if you are using slides. The wonderful thing about wireless clickers is that they allow you to move around the room and be able to control your slide presentation from anywhere. Many of them come with a laser pointer as well, which is useful for highlighting key points on a slide. Take spare batteries if you are taking your own.

Take your own speakers to connect to the laptop if you are playing sound—the experience for the audience is not as good with sound just coming from your laptop, and these days, small speakers are easily available.

Remember your power cable for the laptop—I know, it sounds like I am being overcautious, but then I have seen people's slide deck die right in front of our eyes.

Check to make sure there is enough blank flip chart paper in the room with pens that work. It's always a good idea to keep a pen with you—the ones left in the meeting rooms have usually dried out.

Distractions

Hopefully, you will have rehearsed so well that distractions do not throw you off course. Preparation and rehearsal are like pressure proofing. You have spent time building muscle memory, so that no matter how much pressure you are under on the day, you won't be fazed.

Remember this: the audience's focus will go wherever your attention goes. Common disruptions are things getting dropped or catering staff bringing in tea and coffee into the back of the room. If, for some reason, these incidents catch you off guard and throw you off, take a moment to pause, reset, and carry on. If you don't draw attention to it, the impact is minimized.

If something goes wrong with the slides, rely on your preparation and keep going.

Timing

Your preparation will have set you up quite well in terms of timing—you know how long your talk will last. However, it is helpful to find a way to check on time during your presentation. You could look at your wrist-watch, but that can come across as if you can't wait to finish. Practice doing it in a subtle way. There may be a clock in the room within your line of sight—check it is set to the right time.

Or, ask someone else in the room to give you a five-minute warning—that may well be someone from the conference or events team. Get them to hold up a card with "5 mins" written on it or agree to another signal. Of course, this only works if you remember to look at them.

If you use your own laptop, there is a timer in presenter view. You can also find timer apps for your phone or tablet—countdown timers.

In Chapter 6, we looked at why it is necessary to know timings for each segment of your presentation. If you are in a lineup of speakers, the event organizers will want to know exactly how long you will speak for, so they can organize the whole program.

Getting in the Zone

Presenters have their own individual rituals to get into the right mindset to be ready to present.

Listening to a piece of music that helps you either calm down or get energized is a fantastic way to quickly access a resourceful state. I once coached a partner in a law firm in the preparation for her first multi-speaker conference. She chose a song by Dolly Parton to listen to in the taxi ride to the conference center. I hadn't expected that, but could see why she picked it—definitely an upbeat piece of music!

It might be useful to find a quiet room for one last visualization or some deep breathing and clearing of the mind so you can be present in the moment when you get up to speak.

Seems like an obvious point—you are breathing all the time and know how to do it. Yet, when it comes to nerves and the adrenalin rush, our breathing can quicken and that can result in anxiety. Adrenalin rush is not bad though—it shows you care and are ready to roll. Just focusing on your breath and counting in for four counts then out for four counts a few times can help you slow down your breathing.

When you are about to speak, always take your time to begin—a few seconds to compose yourself. If you are relaxed, then the audience will be too. Look back at the Toastmasters winning speech that Darren Tay gave and watch how he just stands there for a few seconds, taking in the audience while they wait in anticipation (www.youtube.com/watch?v=v26CcifgEq4).

In the same way that your opening needs to be persuasive and strong to engage the audience, it needs to be strong for you, too. Once you get off to a good start, any nerves settle and you have momentum.

If your company is hosting an in-house seminar or you attend another event elsewhere, chatting to members of the audience before the presentations begin is a great way to help you get in the zone. When there are people you do not know who will be in the audience, mingling with them in the networking session beforehand helps you find familiar faces in the crowd later when you speak.

Your Own Feedback

Collecting feedback from the audience is one thing, but what about your own perspective? Capture and find a way to record what was great and what could be improved after every presentation you give. Do it as soon as you can while it is still fresh. Some people keep a small notebook to do this or get someone to record the presentation on a smartphone for them, so they can analyze it later.

Carrying out your own debrief is really useful—it helps you to keep adjusting and improving. Make a commitment to continue toward presentation mastery.

Key Points

- Take your mind map and backup slides on a memory stick with you.
- Take a look at the room in advance.
- Keep handouts back until after the presentation.
- Check AV facilities, including sound for playing video clips and Internet connection.
- Pack spare batteries, cables, pens, and audio speakers.
- Find something to keep you on track with timings.
- Arrive early and find some space to get into the right mindset.

Links

SurveyMonkey
www.surveymonkey.com
Glisser
https://glisser.com
Sli.do
https://www.sli.do
Darren Tay Speech
www.youtube.com/watch?v=v26CcifgEq4

Quick Reference Checklist

Chapter 1

Key Points

- Research company websites and social media profiles to find out areas of interest for your target audience.
- Ask an audience member directly what they want to get out of the presentation
- Think about their motivation for being there.
- Ask yourself: Is what you are intending to share going to be worth their time?

Links

www.linkedin.com

Chapter 2

Key Points

- Start with the end in mind and reverse-engineer your content.
- Set aside time in your calendar to work on your presentation; otherwise, it doesn't happen.
- Use mind mapping to brainstorm your raw data without editing, then leave it for a few days.
- Research industry websites and blogs to find useful material to build into your content.
- Use multisensory material and language to appeal to all sectors of the audience.
- Choose three to five main points only and keep it simple.
- Use the *Why, What, How* format to order your content.
- Craft a strong opening that answers WIIFM.

- End with a clear message—what do you want the audience to
  do or think?

Links

Evernote
https://evernote.com
Useful Business Websites
Entrepreneur.com
Businessinsider.com
www.forbes.com
www.huffingtonpost.co.uk
Harvard Business Review weekly podcast—hbr-ideacast:
https://itunes.apple.com/gb/podcast/hbr-ideacast/id152022135?mt=2
The Monkey Business Illusion
www.youtube.com/watch?v=IGQmdoK_ZfY

Books

Covey, S.R. 2004. *The 7 Habits of Highly Effective People*. New York, NY: Simon
  and Schuster.
Konnikova, M. 2013. *Mastermind: How To Think Like Sherlock Holmes*.
  Edinburgh, UK: Canongate Books Ltd.
Csikszentmihalyi, M. 2008. *Flow*, Harper Perennial Modern Classics.
Knight, S. 2009. *NLP at work*. Nicholas Brearly Publishing.

Chapter 3

Key Points

- Remember that we all learn through stories.
- Start collecting everyday stories from your life.
- Keep stories to one to three minutes.
- Watch TED videos for inspiration and technique.
- Write the story in full and then edit after several days.
- Prepare the story once and use forever.
- Use dialog for your characters to draw in the audience.
- Borrow stories from history or sports.

• Use analogies to compare something complex to something the audience can relate to.

Links

TED
TED.com
Ken Robinson: Do Schools Kill Creativity
www.ted.com/talks/ken_robinson_says_schools_kill_creativity
Darren Tay Toastmaster Winning Speech—excerpt
www.youtube.com/watch?v=v26CcifgEq4
Darren Tay full video within Business Insider article
http://uk.businessinsider.com/toastmasters-public-speaking-champion-darren-tay-2016-8/?r=US&IR=T/#-1

Books

Montefiore, S.S. 2010. *Speeches That Changed The World*. London, UK: Quercus Publishing.
Gray, J. 1999. *Men Are From Mars And Women Are From Venus*. Vermillion.
Covey, S.R., A.R. Merrill, and R.R. Merrill. 1994. *First Things First*. New York, NY: Simon and Schuster.

Chapter 4

Key Points

• Put your data next to an everyday object that the audience knows and can relate to.
• Use flow charts and infographics to show data in a visual way.
• Hold back on detailed data and put it into a handout for later distribution.
• Keep it simple—don't overwhelm the audience with too much data.

Links

Steve Jobs Jan 2008 MacBook Air Video—the relevant part is at about 52 minutes:

www.youtube.com/watch?v=1CgAKBf4bbU
Jill Bolte Taylor: My Stroke of Insight
www.ted.com/talks/jill_bolte_taylor_s_powerful_stroke_of_insight
Canva
www.canva.com

Chapter 5

Key Points

- Use high-quality images to fill the screen, rather than text.
- Keep to one idea per slide.
- Choose font size and style that are easy to read from the back of the room.
- Use flow charts instead of bullet points.
- Group your images so that they stay in place.
- Involve your audience through live polls or quizzes.

Links

Glisser
https://glisser.com
Sli.do
https://www.sli.do
Microsoft Support demonstrating grouping visuals:
https://support.office.com/en-GB/article/Group-or-ungroup-shapes-pictures-or-
    other-objects-a7374c35-20fe-4e0a-9637-7de7d844724b
Microsoft PowerPoint Training:
https://support.office.com/en-gb/article/PowerPoint-training-40e8c930-cb0b-
    40d8-82c4-bd53d3398787?ui=en-US&rs=en-GB&ad=GB

Books

Reynolds, G. 2012. *Presentation Zen.* New Riders.
Resources for images:
www.freedigitalphotos.net
www.gettyimages.co.uk
www.gettyimages.com
www.canva.com

www.presenterme dia.com
https://stocksnap.io

Chapter 6

Key Points

- Find you own authentic style.
- Your words, tone, and body language need to be congruent.
- Practice and shift your mindset to build confidence.
- Be conversational.
- Think about how your body language will be perceived by the audience and adjust your style, if appropriate.

Links

Professor Mehrabian's website:
www.kaaj.com/psych/
Amy Cuddy: Your Body Language Shapes Who You Are:
www.ted.com/talks/amy_cuddy_your_body_language_shapes_who_you_are
Darren Tay full video within Business Insider article:
http://uk.businessinsider.com/toastmasters-public-speaking-champion-darren-
    tay-2016-8/?r=US&IR=T/#-1
Ken Robinson: Do Schools Kill Creativity:
www.ted.com/talks/ken_robinson_says_schools_kill_creativity

Chapter 7

Key Points

- Start observing things that go on around you, in the media, and so on.
- Capture ideas and store them for later.
- Keep editing your humorous story until you get to the punch-line as quickly as you can.
- Add an element of surprise or misdirection to get you to the punchline.
- Use pictures and video to add humor.

Links

Steve Jobs calling Starbucks—the relevant part is at about 46 minutes into this
video:
www.youtube.com/watch?v=mqylGY_YSXA
Sir Ken Robinson
www.ted.com/talks/ken_robinson_says_schools_kill_creativity
Darren Tay, World Champion—Toastmasters Speech Contest 2016
http://uk.businessinsider.com/toastmasters-public-speaking-champion-darren-
tay-2016-8/?r=US&IR=T/#-1

Chapter 8

Key Points

- Rehearse to feel more confident and remember your material
better.
- Record your rehearsal on a video, so that you can see and hear
what the audience will experience.
- Practice in front of colleagues and test out tough questions
the audience might ask.
- Try the visualization technique to help with confidence.
- Use the memory palace technique to remember your key
points.
- Know the timings of every segment of your talk, so that you
know where to cut on short notice.

Links

Harvard Medical Magazine
https://hms.harvard.edu/news/harvard-medicine/harvard-medicine/play/
competitive-edge
Toastmasters International
www.toastmasters.org

Books

Gawain, S. 2002. *Creative Visualization*. Uttarakhand, India: Natraj Publishing.
Phelps, M., and A. Abrahamson. 2008. *No Limits*. New York, NY: Simon and
Schuster.

Chapter 9

Key Points

- Think of questions as an opportunity for you to showcase your expertise.
- Remember, it is an opportunity for the audience to get their questions answered—put yourself in their shoes to anticipate what kind of questions could come up.
- Use your mind map from the brainstorming phase to help you prepare for questions.
- Rehearse taking questions and decide when or if you will take them, so you can let the audience know up front.
- Practice your version of "I don't know," so that you can feel confident and not worry about getting caught.

Chapter 10

Key Points

- Printed slides don't mean anything without you, the presenter, explaining them, so ditch those types of handouts.
- Prepare a report or article instead of printing hard copies of your slides.
- E-mail the report after the event to create another touch point and remain in front of mind.
- Use printed hard copies of charts and spreadsheets where the data is too small to read on the screen.

Chapter 11

Key Points

- Take your mind map and backup slides on a memory stick with you.
- Take a look at the room in advance.
- Keep handouts back until after the presentation.
- Check AV facilities, including sound for playing video clips and Internet connection.

- Pack spare batteries, cables, pens, and audio speakers.
- Find something to keep you on track with timings.
- Arrive early and find some space to get into the right mindset.

Links

SurveyMonkey
www.surveymonkey.com
Glisser
https://glisser.com
Sli.do
https://www.sli.do
Darren Tay Speech
www.youtube.com/watch?v=v26CcifgEq4

Index

OTHER TITLES IN OUR CORPORATE COMMUNICATION COLLECTION

Debbie DuFrene, Stephen F. Austin State University, Editor

- *Technical Marketing Communication: A Guide to Writing, Design, and Delivery* by Emil B. Towner and Heidi L. Everett
- *Communication for Consultants* by Rita R. Owens
- *Zen and the Art of Business Communication: A Step-by-Step Guide to Improving Your Business Writing Skills* by Susan L. Luck
- *The Essential Guide to Business Communication for Finance Professionals* by Jason L. Snyder and Lisa A.C. Frank
- *Planning and Organizing Business Reports: Written, Oral, and Research-Based* by Dorinda Clippinger
- *Producing Written and Oral Business Reports: Formatting, Illustrating, and Presenting* by Dorinda Clippinger
- *How to Write Brilliant Business Blogs, Volume I: The Skills and Techniques You Need* by Suzan St. Maur
- *How to Write Brilliant Business Blogs, Volume II: What to Write About* by Suzan St. Maur

Announcing the Business Expert Press Digital Library

Concise e-books business students need for classroom and research

This book can also be purchased in an e-book collection by your library as

- a one-time purchase,
- that is owned forever,
- allows for simultaneous readers,
- has no restrictions on printing, and
- can be downloaded as PDFs from within the library community.

Our digital library collections are a great solution to beat the rising cost of textbooks. E-books can be loaded into their course management systems or onto students' e-book readers.
The **Business Expert Press** digital libraries are very affordable, with no obligation to buy in future years. For more information, please visit **www.businessexpertpress.com/librarians**. To set up a trial in the United States, please email **sales@businessexpertpress.com**.

www.ingramcontent.com/pod-product-compliance
Lightning Source LLC
Chambersburg PA
CBHW062014200326
41519CB00017B/4800